MARKETING M

An Introduction to t. ... Communications in Marketing

About the Author

Dr Leslie Gofton is Lecturer in Behavioural Science at the University of Newcastle-upon-Tyne. He has published several books and articles on marketing topics over the course of a 20-year career in teaching, research and consultancy. His real loves, however, are his family and playing blues guitar.

Marketing Messages

*An Introduction to the Study of
Communications in Marketing*

LR Gofton

BLACKHALL
Publishing

This book was typeset by Gilbert Composing for

BLACKHALL PUBLISHING
26 Eustace Street
Dublin 2
Ireland

e-mail: blackhall@tinet.ie

ISBN: 1 901657 26 4

A catalogue record for this book is available from the British Library.

Printed in Ireland by
ColourBooks Ltd

CONTENTS

To Celia, Peter and Lauren,
who gave me the reason to write books,
and to my dear mother,
Joan McLean Gofton,
who gave me a voice to begin with . . .

INTRODUCTION

The person on the Clapham Omnibus, although surrounded by marketing communications, and certain of their unsavoury intentions, would invariably deny being affected by them. Advertising, most of us are sure, influences other people, although no one is exactly sure who they might be. This common suspicion of advertising and other aspects of marketing activity almost certainly springs from the idea that they involve 'mind bending' and various kinds of 'hidden persuaders' to borrow the title of Vance Packard's famous 'expose' of promotional villainy, published in the early-1960s. When marketers communicate, most people think, they are usually up to no good, and all they really want to do is sell us something we don't really need.

One of the purposes of this book is to dispel this mis-apprehension. Marketing communications, the subject of the book, are varied in form and intention. Consumers are now more experienced and sophisticated than at any time in the past – saturated product markets and the proliferation of media communicating with these consumers means that, in order to compete, many different kinds of marketing objectives need to be pursued, according to the specific conditions and problems facing the individual product, or service, as it moves through the stages of the product life cycle. Thus marketing communications have become increasingly varied in form and intention; if Packard's world of media-manipulated puppets ever existed, it is surely long gone.

This book will explain what marketing communication is, and illustrate the how it fits into the marketing mix. As we shall see, this involves many varied forms, from the different kinds of advertising media and messages employed by different products and services, through the image building of specialist types of communication, such as sponsorship and public relations, to include the important strategic communication objectives pursued through branding, logos and trade names, packaging, product placement, and so on. In order to reinforce the learning messages in the main text, each chapter ends with a number of cases, based closely on real brands and their problems. Students are advised to try to answer the questions set in order to make the most of the chapter.

I can only aim to provide a general overview and a concise but informative introduction in a text such as this, and students are recommended to pursue specialist aspects of this topic through the many excellent journals and texts constantly increasing the depth of coverage offered in this field. I hope that this text will change the way you think about the role of communication in the marketing process.

Dr Leslie Gofton
July 1999

Dr Leslie Ross Gofton
Department of Social Policy
University of Newcastle
Claremont Road
Newcastle-upon-Tyne
NE1 7RU

1

MARKETING AND ITS MESSAGES: INTEGRATED MARKETING COMMUNICATIONS

Introducing the Marketing Mix

'Marketing communications' is the term applied to a range of techniques and processes by marketers and companies selling goods and services to transmit and receive information. This in itself tells us little about those processes and techniques. However, in order to understand what is done, by whom and why, we need to fit this into the context in which it takes place.

Marketing communications take place within the marketing mix and can be said to comprise a further 'mix' of elements. To understand what the *communications mix* is trying to accomplish, it is essential to recall the main reason for marketing at all.

Marketing is the management process responsible for identifying, anticipating and satisfying customer requirements at a profit. Broadly speaking, marketing is concerned with the relationship between the management system producing goods, and making them available, and the consumers at whom they are directed. This involves a range of issues, depending on the goods and the nature of the markets concerned, which include:

- the kind of profit sought (note that some goods and services do not seek a commercial profit, for example, charities and social services);
- customer needs;
- how to gain customer loyalty/brand loyalty;
- how to ensure repeat purchases.

Marketing is concerned with four or five main 'ingredients': what is called the 'marketing mix'. These are aspects of the way the product is produced and made available to the consumer and are typically represented through the following.

- Product (the physical form, and its characteristics).
- Price (what it charged for the product).
- Place (where the product can be bought or obtained).
- Promotion.

This last ingredient will be one of the major topics of this book. It comprises the variety of ways the product and its attributes are communicated to the consumer. These include:

- selling;
- advertising;
- sales promotion;
- direct marketing;
- publicity and public relations;
- sponsorship;
- exhibitions;
- corporate image making;
- packaging;
- point-of-sale material and merchandising activity;
- informally, by 'word of mouth'.

Which of these areas is considered important, and made the subject of a strategic move, is dependent on the context and the nature of the marketing problem. Clearly, industrial marketers place much heavier emphasis on personal selling than do 'fast moving consumer goods' (FMCG) manufacturers, since the products and their markets are entirely different.

Promotion, Communicating and Marketing – Key Terms and their Definitions

What is Promotion?

Promotion is concerned with communication between the seller and the buyer and is controlled by the seller who seeks to promote his products. The different methods involved are:

- advertising (above-the-line activities);
- sales and promotion activities (below-the-line activities);
- publicity or public relations;
- sales force activities.

The way these are combined is called the *communications mix*. This varies according to the nature of the product, market conditions and customer. Industrial markets, for example, tend to rely on personal selling because there are a small number of customers, whereas FMCG manufacturers use advertising and sales promotion to reach a greater number of potential buyers. *Advertising* is "purposive communication" – drawing attention to the characteristics of a product that will appeal to the buying motives of customers in the *target segment* of the market. It aims to identify the exploitable characteristic (in marketing terms, what distinguishes it from other products), either in the *form* of the product, or in the *brand image* which is promoted, and to communicate this in the form of a 'selling proposition' to the target group. According to Philip Kotler, one of the foremost marketing gurus:

> *The purpose of advertising is to enhance potential buyers' responses to the organisation and its offerings. It seeks to do so by providing information, by trying to channelise desires and by supplying reasons for preferring the particular organisation's offerings.*

Marketing communications typically involve two main kinds of activity.

- **Below-the-line promotion**: indirect promotional expenditure, such as publicity or public relations.
- **Above-the-line promotion**: such as direct advertising.

Below-the-line Promotions

> *All non-media promotion. (Christopher)*

> *...the supplementary selling activity co-ordinates personal selling and advertising into an effective persuasive force. (Engel et al)*

The term 'line' was used originally by advertising agencies to distinguish between promotional, commissionable expenditures – i.e. those the agency had to pay for, or commission – and non-commissionable expenditures. However, it assumes a false dichotomy. Differences in kinds of advertising expenditure are not generally so clear cut and should not be over emphasised. A *total* approach is needed, rather than looking at the differences between the types of expenditure emphasising the distinctions between the forms of activity involved.

A useful distinction is often made between those promotions aiming to move products from the marketing channel intermediary and those aimed at moving the product from the manufacturers into the channel of distribution ('pull' and 'push' promotional techniques respectively). *Pull* refers to the use of consumer incentives and *push* to the use of trade and sales force incentives.

Above-the-line Promotions

Above-the-line refers to any promotional activity which involves a commission – that is, activity in which payment is involved for the communication which takes place. The various forms of advertising are the obvious example: the agencies producing advertisements on television or in the print media are paid, the media they employ charge for the time space and effort involved in 'running' the advertisement, and the recipients are well aware that this is kind of communication is 'advertiser dominated', so that credibility is always problematic, and customers expect the content of such communications to be biased and partial.

Three Main Types of Advertising

Advertising is a diverse form of activity but can be broadly classified into three types.

1.　　**Informative advertising**: conveying information, raising awareness. Used in early stages of the product life cycle (PLC).
2.　　**Persuasive advertising**: creating desire, stimulating purchase. Highly competitive, used in growth/maturity stages of the PLC.
3.　　**Reminding advertising**: used for well-established products, reminding about the existence, benefits, characteristics, reinforcing existing knowledge.

We can distinguish also between *brand* advertising and *generic* advertising. The former aims to increase the sales of one manufacturer's brand of a particular product, while the latter is concerned to increase sales of a particular type of product. Generic advertising may be used when a product type is very new, with little in the way of competition between brands, and also in areas where branding is not significant (e.g. in basic product areas, such as certain kinds of food products).

Advertising Objectives

General objectives include:

- to ensure a certain exposure for the advertised product or service;
- to create awareness of new products or developments to existing products;
- to improve customer attitudes towards the product or the firm;

- to increase sales (although it is difficult to relate advertising to sales volume) and profits. For a non-profit organisation, the equivalent purpose will be to increase response to the product or service;
- to generate enquiries from potential customers;
- to change the attitudes and habits of people at whom the advertisement is directed. Much government advertising aims to do this (e.g. drink driving, anti-smoking).

It is important to distinguish between long-term and short-term effects.

Specific objectives might include:

- communicating information;
- highlighting specific features or communicating the *unique selling proposition* (USP);
- building brand or corporate image;
- reinforcing customer behaviour;
- influencing dealers or re-sellers to stock the item;
- achieving a policy objective (e.g. government advertising).

The role of advertising in the *industrial* marketing is, however, very different. The objectives it might pursue could include:

- awareness building;
- comprehension building;
- efficient reminding;
- lead generation;
- legitimation;
- reassurance.

Planning a Promotion Campaign

This involves six main steps.

1. **Identifying the target audience**.
    This requires the specification of relevant audience characteristics. For consumer goods and services this specification will be in terms of social and psycho-social features; for industrial goods this will be in terms of commercial and economic aspects.

2. **Specifying the promotional image we will seek to communicate.**
    The bases for audience selectivity (why particular audiences are sought) will need to be specified, while at the same time clearly defining the objectives, the

audience, etc.

Since it is very likely that each campaign will involve a different combination of factors, the importance of the different functions of the campaign will need to be specified, as will the types of appeal to be used.

3.   **Selecting the media.**

4.   **Preparing schedules for the use of media.**

5.   **Setting the promotional budget.**
        This will be directly derived from the overall strategic plan prepared by the company as the basis for a specific product.

6.   **Looking at the effectiveness of the promotional and communicational techniques and evaluating the number of strategic objectives that have been realised.**

Branding

Branding is a very general term covering brand names, designs, trademarks, symbols, jingles and the like. A brand name refers strictly to letters, words or groups of words. A brand image distinguishes a company's product from competing products in the eye of the user.

In brand identity, names are linked with those visual features assisting in stimulating demand for a particular product. These may include typography, colour, package design and slogans.

The Reasons for Branding

The main reasons for branding include:

- product differentiation, identifying the product, increasing loyalty;
- creating separate product identity;
- improving acceptance by wholesalers and retailers;
- facilitating self-selection in self-service stores;
- reducing the importance of price differentials.

Brand loyalty in customers gives a manufacturer more control over marketing strategy and the choice of channels of distribution. It also permits the 'piggy backing' of new goods, developing new products on the basis of existing brand names. This is referred to as a 'brand extension' strategy. It also eases the task of personal selling and makes market segmentation easier.

Branding is not, however, equally relevant for all types of product or for all customers. For example, when brand loyalty is likely to be low (e.g. for low cost or infrequently purchased products or for products bought by infrequent shoppers) or where the brand is likely to be of little importance in terms of status or display features (e.g. in the brand of air conditioning installed in a house). Note also the importance of quality control in living up to a promoted image of quality.

Branding strategies include:

- **Family branding**: where a group of related products all use the same brand name.
- **Brand extension**: where a range of products are built upon the basis of a brand name associated with a single product, or product type.
- **Multi-branding**: where the products manufactured by a particular company are all marketed using different brand names (e.g. products made by Procter & Gamble in the USA and the UK). This is sometimes known as the 'fighting brands' approach.

  Various *communications strategies* are involved. Family branding aims to develop consumer confidence and familiarity, and to build up image characteristics and attributes, such as quality associated with a particular brand name. This will then be conveyed to all products carrying that brand name. Multi-branding aims to maximise brand sales by emphasising the uniqueness and distinctive advantages in each of the brands.

  This, however, must be done carefully since there are some very famous examples of attempted uses of brand names with products which have been inappropriate or ill-judged for a variety of reasons. For example, the denim leisure-clothing manufacturer Levi-Strauss attempted to market a range of formal suits and footwear under the family brand name. Not only did the products fail to sell, since customers did not relate the brand name to this type of product, but it also proved damaging to the established brand name and the products were hastily withdrawn from the market.

- **Trade marks**: A legal term covering words and symbols. Trade marks are an extremely important part of the branding process and a well-established brand will usually develop a familiar trade mark. This is a very valuable item and the ownership of such trade marks is very jealously guarded. This is because of the powerful communicative effects trade marks can produce. Many have been built up over a long period of time and have created strong consumer loyalty. McDonald's, for example, have control over very large numbers of words and symbols associated with the company's image and brand, including 'Mc', McDonald's, the Arches, red and yellow in restaurant colours and a whole range of other 'intellectual property'. They consider this to be essential in order to protect the image and standards on which the success of the franchise is based.

Sales Promotion

Non-media advertising and 'below-the-line' advertising (or activities) are alternative terms which mean sales promotion activities. Sales promotions are used extensively, because there is often a direct link between the promotion and short-term sales volume, e.g. reduced price bargains, free gift offers or competitions.

Sales promotional techniques may be concerned with a number of different ends, e.g. inducing trials, affecting usage behaviour, creating 'switching' from one brand to another or preventing it.

Consumer promotions might involve the following very familiar techniques:

- free samples;
- coupon offers ('money off' offers);
- price reductions;
- competitions;
- free gifts;
- combination pack offers;
- off-price labels;
- trading stamps;
- exhibitions and demonstrations;
- catalogues;
- on-pack offers.

Retailer or middleman promotions may also be used. These are part of a 'push' policy. Examples here might include:

- extending credit;

- merchandising facilities;
- contests for retailers or shop assistants.

Consumer promotion and advertising act as a 'pull policy' to attract dealer attention by increasing consumer demand. Other techniques might include:

- sales force promotions;
- industrial promotions.

Objectives of Sales Promotions

These are essentially short-term measures, with broadly similar objectives to above-the-line techniques. The overriding aims are, at the end of the day, to increase sales, by generating extra interest, to attract new customers, to encourage retailers to stock more of the items, to encourage slow moving lines and to clear out stocks. It is also important to counter the moves of any competing products, establish new products and encourage the sales force to greater effort.

This might involve, for example, encouraging current non-users to undertake a trial or getting existing customers to increase the frequency, or the volume, of the purchases that they make. Switching, or persuading, users of rival brands to move to the brand in question, is also a common aim.

Types of Sales Promotion

1.   **Merchandising**
      Typically, manufacturers rely on re-seller organisations to get goods to customers. Merchandising is a method the manufacturer tries to ensure that a retailer sells as many of his products as quickly as possible. The manufacturer therefore gives advice to the retailer, either from the sales force or from full-time merchandising specialists. Merchandising is concerned with putting the manufacturer's goods in the right place at the right time. This would involve considering issues, such as:

      - right stores, right positions within stores;
      - times of peak demand (e.g. Christmas, particular weekdays);
      - providing staff to demonstrate products;
      - point-of-sale material.

Examples of point-of-sale material might include the

following: posters, showcards, mobiles, dump bins, dummy packs, bags, stands and also 'crowners', i.e. tags or slogans slipped over the neck of a bottle.

Sales literature and exhibitions and trade fairs may also be important in achieving marketing objectives relating to retailers.

2.   **Publicity**
Publicity is defined as being any form of non-paid, non-personal communication and, like advertising, it involves dealing with a mass audience. Although some components are 'paid for', we can also include public relations under this general heading, since it is concerned more generally with building and maintaining an understanding between the organisation and the general public. Benefits of good publicity include:

- image building;
- no major time costs;
- access to large audiences;
- high message credibility.

Problems include the fact that publicity is difficult to control. Press releases may not be reported in the way intended and sponsorship may not achieve the communications objectives concerned. It may, for example, improve distributor and customer relations, modify the attitudes of potential customers, develop corporate citizenship or promote a particular public image, but there are difficulties surrounding the effects achieved. There may, on occasion, be unintended side effects or unanticipated results.

The marketing communications mix involves the unique blend of these devices, used to accomplish the marketing objectives required in this particular situation.

3.   **Above and below-the-line activity**
The 'line' referred to is derived from the old way commission payment was presented in accounts. Advertising involving payment of a commission for the purchase of space or time, was considered to be 'above-the-line'. Other communication tools (e.g. in-store activity involved in merchandising or public relations) since they did not require the payment of a commission,

were considered to be 'below-the-line'. The exception is personal selling, which does not fit into either category.

4. **Push and pull**

It is also common to describe the way the marketing strategy operates in terms of 'push' or 'pull'. A *push* strategy, for example, will be driven by sales force activity, backed up by trade promotions: the product is said to be 'pushed' in order to achieve shelf space in as many outlets as possible. *Pull* aims to attract customers into the stores. The classic way to achieve this is through advertising to increase demand. In practice, of course, these two types of approach are almost always strongly complementary, although it may be appropriate to focus on one or the other approach according to the stage at which the product finds itself.

The effectiveness of such programmes is nevertheless dependent on the degree of synergy with the other dimensions of the marketing activity achieved by even the most effective marketing communication programme, for example, the price charged or the distribution strategy followed.

The Effectiveness of Integrated Marketing Communications

The essential achievement of the effective communications mix is to realise the complete harmonisation of activity in each of the communication mix areas so as to achieve the common goal. It is essential that each aspect of the mix should be integrated with every other aspect. For example:

- **advertising** supported and complemented by public relations;
- **sales promotion** closely geared to the activities of both advertising and public relations experts;
- **above and below-the-line activities** working smoothly towards the same objectives;
- **sales contacts** being used, for example, to enhance direct selling through the use of customer databases;
- **promotion** being achieved through the messages contained on packaging;
- **point-of-sale promotions** enhancing the effect of advertising by following through on the messages involved.

Maximum impact may be achieved by drawing together the effects of all the marketing communications tools involved. Thus, for example, if all the graphic work is fully integrated throughout the planning and design stages, then the message will be more effectively communicated and the costs will be considerably improved. For specific types of work, new ideas may be brought in through involving different creative teams at various points in the process of building up the communications mix. This, however, may be more expensive.

'Blanket' Approaches to Marketing Communications

Careful use of 'buying models' will enable the marketer to identify the key elements in the communications mix. Blanket, or saturation coverage of all the communication channels relevant to a particular target market, will then increase the likelihood of achieving marketing objectives.

Reaching a proportion of the target group is sometimes referred to as achieving a particular 'share of mind'. In the case of blanket coverage, the expectation is that the higher the spend on various aspects of the marketing mix, the greater the 'share of mind' that will be achieved. Other marketing communications campaigns may aim to maintain the level of awareness a company has, this is referred to as keeping the product or brand in 'front-of-mind awareness'. The 'physical' metaphor is maintained in that advertising expenditure as a proportion of total marketing spend, for example, is often referred to as 'share of voice'.

The importance of 'spend', and the effectiveness of blanket or saturation coverage can be testified by the effectiveness of advertising by companies such as McDonald's. They employ this high level of expenditure on marketing communication channels to their target groups and also, in the case of campaigns and merchandising, linking films with related product areas, such as soft drinks, toys, children's food, music and television programmes. In many cases, *product placement* deals are negotiated by large companies who agree to underwrite significant parts of the cost of films on condition that their products are featured and mentioned in specific scenes (e.g. Pepsi in the *Back to the Future* series or Mercedes in *The Lost World*).

> *Test cases at the end of each chapter provide the opportunity to try out some of the ideas to which you have just been introduced and to apply some of the practical techniques of marketing communications.*

MARKETING FINANCIAL SERVICES

Norman Wilbur, MD, Floyds Bank plc: an address to the coming changes

In the new millennium branch personnel are the key. They are the ones who have to deal with the public and how the public thinks of the company will depend on these contacts. Present practices are expensive and, for many of those concerned, onerous. Many of the most time consuming activities, which are also the most costly, are simply routine. Although sales and marketing are becoming more important, less than one third of expenditure is on this function. As customer needs become more complex it is more and more difficult to meet them from the old-style bank branch. (Norman Wilbur, MD Floyds Bank, at the 'Towards 2000' conference)

My job as Floyds MD involves a great many different responsibilities, but I have recently come to the realisation that marketing is actually the key to the future success of the company and I have decided to do something about it. Much of my time at the bank is actually spent in the branches and this more than anything else brings home to me the importance of good marketing and an effective policy with regard to the selling of our financial services. It isn't my own special area and it has brought home to me the kind of perspective we need to adopt for the future success of the bank.

What does this new perspective involve?

Our bank, like most organisations, is confronted with the problem of reaching and selling to markets and customers that have changed a great deal over the past few years; their wants and needs are certainly different. Reaching these customers involves competitive thinking and developing an 'offer' that beats our competitors. We need a distinctive edge – what the marketing people call a 'competitive advantage'.

Make no mistake, this is a matter of commercial life and death. We sink or swim on our ability to compete and the number of failures we have seen in this sector over the past few years should leave none of you in any doubt that this is simply hyperbole born out of a pep talk. If our organisation fails to deliver what the customer wants, at the quality they demand, at the price they are prepared to pay (and, of course, at a profit) we are dead meat.

A team effort

This is what marketing is about, but it isn't down to the marketing department alone; it is everybody's job. From board level down to the most junior employee in the smallest branch, this is what we must take as our focus. If we fail to deliver good personal service, or develop a weakness compared to our competitors, in the offer we make to the customer, we are going to pay for it in profits and consequently in the jobs, wages and conditions we can offer to our staff. Marketing staff will, from now on, be making regular visits to every branch, to make sure you are aware of policies and strategies the company is following and precisely what your role is within those activities.

This is a two-way process, however. When these teams visit the branches, they are also getting feedback from you. The marketing programme means nothing without input from the staff for whom it is such an important matter. You are our contacts with the customer and without this input of the consumer perspective, we are most likely to end up pursuing the wrong aims.

Market research is essential; this information is the lifeblood of our company and, as well as this vital feedback from your contacts with the customers, our market research activity will be focused on providing relevant and comprehensive data, which can be used by personnel at all levels within the organisation. Our new management information system, *Floydata*, is coming on stream within the next six months and all personnel will be provided with the opportunity to acquire the skills which will enable them to make the maximum use of its potential. All this is directed toward knowing our customer as comprehensively as we possibly can. We need to know what they want and you are a vital component in both the gathering of such information and the implementation of programmes designed to meet those needs.

We also, of course, need financial products we can sell. We must have financial services relevant to the needs of the customer as they come into your branches day in, day out. You must understand these products and be able to sell them effectively, but you must also understand that, although branches will continue to be important, there will be an increasingly important role for new mechanisms to reach the customer. Our distribution system will be much more varied in the future and we need all our staff to know what it is and what it can do.

It is vital that all aspects of our marketing effort should be closely synchronized and co-ordinated. Our advertising (including television, both terrestrial and satellite, as well as press, cinema and, increasingly, the internet) must pull in the same direction as staff policies and the advertising and promotional activity we operate within the branches.

Above all, we need to communicate with the customer. If they do not know about our services, or do not properly understand them, they will not make use of them. They must be reached! In the past, these activities have not always been successful. In some cases, this is because the policies have been wrong, but often, it represents a failure on the part of those charged with making them work, from the highest levels within the company down to the customer interface. Our new marketing team, drawn from the best personnel presently in the company, but also strengthened by vigorous recruitment to draw in the best people in the industry, will pursue a new set of company goals. I believe we can express the underlying principles succinctly; they are an attempt to form a vision for the next century.

We cannot simply carry on doing what we already do: that way we would find ourselves expending ever more energy on simply staying where we are – or even falling behind in spite of desperate activity and sacrifice. Our watchwords must be simplicity, selectivity and quality. *Simplicity* because we will only succeed if we do more of those things we do best and generate the most profit. *Selectivity* because we need to discard all those activities which are not central, 'core' business and *quality* because that is the only way we can satisfy our customers in the global high street, in the face of keen and growing competition from every side.

Success is there to be had. Success, however, comes from people and the challenge for Floyds is to use our most important resource – you – in the most effective way. The new century will, I believe, mark the beginning of a golden age for this organisation, but we can only make it happen together.

1.1 *What is the 'marketing task' as perceived by Wilbur? Critically evaluate the way in which he sees marketing, introducing as many other components as you can think of.*

1.2 *Why is good marketing essential to the future success of Floyds Bank? What role will branch personnel play in the marketing-driven company?*

1.3 *What will be the advantages of recruiting key marketing staff from outside the banking sector? What will be the disadvantages?*

1.4 *Using the example of your own organisation, or an organisation that you know well, consider the ways that organisation:*
a) impresses upon you the advantages of good marketing;
b) informs you of your personal role in the implementation of good marketing policy.

After describing these processes, write down the ways you think your own company's application of marketing principles could be improved (or those of a business you know about).

1.5 *Consider the ways this strategy may affect the development of Floyds' marketing plans and outline the main limitations that may consequently arise.*

1.6 *What are the main differences between the marketing of goods and the marketing of services? Is this fully reflected in Floyds' marketing strategy?*

EVERYONE'S FAVOURITE GETS A NEW LOOK

The nation's favourite chocolates, *Kwality Road*, are to be revamped in the most expensive operation of its type since the brand first appeared more than half a century ago. The new look will appear on confectioners' shelves in the late autumn, in the run up to the busiest chocolate-eating part of the year – the Christmas season. It is understood that the new look will involve a completely revamped assortment and redesigns for the bags, cartons and tins that have become such a familiar feature of sweet shops throughout the nation. In addition, a huge campaign of advertising and promotion will take place, including newly commissioned posters, television advertising and a 500,000 consumer promotion campaign targeting supermarkets and grocery stores as well as the newsagents and corner shops, which are so important in the marketing of this product.

The re-launch is felt to be needed because of falling market share in the face of competition and the recognition that the brand is now thought to be 'old fashioned' by the younger consumers who are such heavy consumers of chocolate products. Brand manager Crispin Shaker commented:

> *The company intends to increase the numbers of preferred, favourite sweets, such as the noisette triangle and toffee nut cream. Our research programme has indicated what works and what doesn't in the existing product. Although these*

changes are more than a 'tweak', we will be keeping those aspects of the existing product and marketing mix that we know to be liked and valued by our existing, highly brand-loyal, consumer base. Existing cardboard boxes will be replaced by new shapes with transparent film windows and the entire range of Kwality Road jars, packs and tins will feature the new colour scheme of white on purple, rather than the existing purple on white, which was introduced in 1961.

We feel this gives the product a more contemporary style but we will be keeping our trademarks, Miss Kwality and Captain Roads. These have come to embody the image and brand values for which we are known – traditional quality and reliability.

Wrapper colours will stay the same, since these were highly rated in consumer research because of their bright colours, originality and quality feeling when handled. Mr Shaker commented that these were substantial changes to take account of consumer needs and preferences.

Kwality Road was still the gift and purchase of choice at the Christmas period, but was no longer competing effectively with the romantic image cultivated by competitors, such as the new Belgian brands coming into the UK. One important aspect of the re-launch will be a huge mail drop which will invite householders throughout the UK to "find Miss Kwality" under a number of scratch panels. Winners will be offered the choice of cash, holidays or a car and every one of the hundred winners will receive a box of *Kwality Road* every Christmas for the rest of their lives. Two thousand runners up will get a consolation box of chocolates – *Kwality Road*, of course!

1.7   *What is a re-launch? Why is it necessary in this case?*

1.8   *What is 'the marketing mix'? Using the Kwality Road case as an example, explain how the marketing mix has been changed in this case.*

1.9   *What factors in consumer use of chocolates and related behaviour are likely to affect the market for this product? How might these factors be influenced by marketing activity?*

1.10   *Identify the various factors that are likely to be included in a communications mix for Kwality Road. Draw up a plan, with justifications, suggesting an appropriate set of strategies for the communications and promotional activities the company is likely to pursue.*

1.11   *Consider a product/service marketed either by your organisation or one with which you are familiar. Describe each element of the marketing mix involved. Say how, in your opinion, these elements might be changed to make the marketing of the product more effectively.*

2
COMMUNICATIONS FACTORS

Models of Marketing Communication

In order to fully appreciate how the marketing communication process works, it is essential to have a good understanding of the main dimensions of communication and what factors are likely to be important in transmitting and receiving marketing information.

Communication is the process by which individuals share meaning. For it to be successful, it is necessary that information should be transmitted. This can be regarded in a number of different ways.

- **As a *negotiation* between individuals**: here persuasion involves a variety of overt rewards and punishments.
- **As *propaganda***: target audiences are subject to the influence process by means of symbols, training and cultural indoctrination.
- **As a *speaker* addressing a large group**: attempting to achieve influence through the structure of material, the manner of delivery and the form of evidence.

A number of different models have been put forward in the attempt to represent how communication takes place. We shall review some of the most influential, in relation to the study of marketing communications.

Schramm's Linear Model of Communication

Schramm sees communication as involving the transmission of information in a linear process. That is to say, the elements follow one another in a sequence. He considers the best elements to be the following.

Source, the Communicator

This may be an individual or an organisation. This is where

the need to transmit information originates and this is where the medium (the words, images, sounds, smells or other symbolic means in which it is to be conveyed) are selected. The use of sportsmen or television celebrities in order to convey messages indicates how important this can be. Also, the use of symbols to convey authority in spokespersons ('lab' coats, black-rimmed spectacles, to convey 'science' or 'expertise') is very common.

The Encoding Process

This is part of the process of communication in itself and is particularly important for a number of reasons.

- **The capacity of the target group to understand**: the communication may be misread by the source of the communication and, as a consequence, the process of encoding may actually influence the way the message is interpreted.
- **The source may be perceived as biased by the target group**: as wrong or distorted and so this will affect the way the message is interpreted.
- **The means by which the message is communicated (e.g. sales staff)**: this may lead to the misinterpretation of the message.

Thus the encoding process must be seen as a factor in itself and not a neutral aspect of the process of communication.

Message or Signal

This may be oral, written, verbal or non-verbal in a symbol or a sign. A *channel* is the means by which the message is transmitted. This may involve direct, face to face contact and word-of-mouth or mass communication, which is indirect and involves non-personal contact through media, such as the press, the mail, electronic communication or posters. Personal communication processes are more powerful and effective, because of the richness and flexibility in the modes of delivery of the message.

Decoding Process

This is the process of interpreting and understanding the message. This is influenced by the characteristics of the message itself, including the source, the context and the cultural, social, psychological and physical characteristics of the receiving individual.

Destination or Receiver

As the above makes clear, the receiver is an active component in the process, interpreting, making inferences and attributing characteristics on the basis of perceptions of the message source – the medium, the content, the context, etc.

These involve a linear sequence. However, there is also a *feedback* loop between the beginning and ending of the sequence and *noise* factors involved in the transmission process, which are likely to be significant.

Figure 2.1: Linear Communication Process

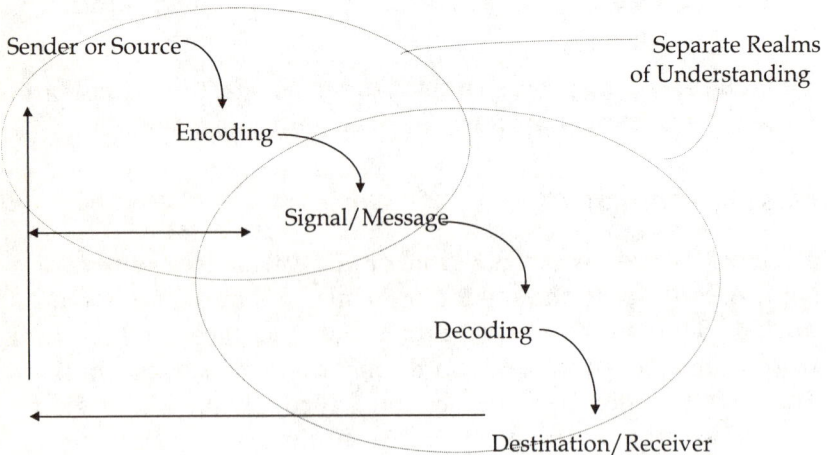

Transmitting the Marketing Concept and Communicating Product Features Involves Encoding into Symbols

It is essential that the form of the message should be appropriate. Even with something as basic as the wording of a slogan, it cannot simply be assumed that all the words used convey the same thing to each person in the audience. Images may be con-ventional, but may be boring, ineffective or even offensive to the target audience. It is therefore essential to consider the importance of the symbolic power of advertising and to consider the different ways communication takes place.

Communication to Target Audiences via Channels

Sensory channels (sight, sound, smell, touch and taste) are the ultimate means by which information is received.

These are usually interrelated although the dominant mode of receiving information is sight, followed by sound. Other ways in which information is received include the following.

- **Non-verbal communication**: this would include aspects such as kinetics ('body language') and proxemics (the use and occupation of space, how we stand in and move about in space, social space, etc.).
- **Non-symbolic communication**: this would include 'instinctual' reactions to body signs, such as smells (hormonal levels) eye movements, body shapes, etc. We may also react instinctually to certain settings (e.g. spaces and sounds) or shapes and designs (stimulating threat responses, etc.).
- **Semiotics**: this involves the study of how symbols and signs are used in communication. Interpreting advertising involves target consumers using rich and complex resources in order to generate meaning. These are part of the common, everyday practices used by consumers in order to make sense of what is going on around them.

  Any culture is built around symbols, interpreted by members of the culture using similar sets of experiences and understandings. Advertisers themselves establish symbols in, for example, the communication of 'brand personality'. A famous example, in the UK, is the 'embodiment' of brand personality of Guinness stout into the central character of a series of advertisements, played by the actor Rutger Hauer.

Feedback to the original communicator is an important aspect of the communication process. In some marketing communications, it may well be a crucial and central element. In face to face contact (e.g. between a salesman and a customer) this is instantaneous and part of the art of salesmanship involves monitoring and responding to such feedback sequences.

In mass communication, this is much more problematic. Marketing research seeks to devise:

- ways of gathering up feedback signals (including, customer complaints, word of mouth responses, etc.);
- ways in which reactions to aspects of the communications mix can be monitored (e.g. tests of recall, laboratory techniques to monitor customer scanning of advertising messages, focus group tests, telephone surveys, etc.).

Figure 2.2: One-step Flow of Communication

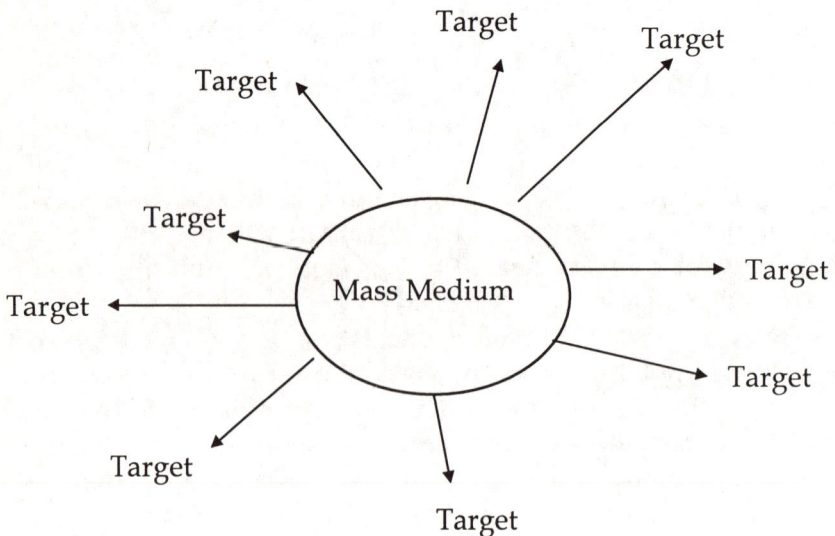

Mass Communication Models

Mass communication still represents the most cost-effective method of communication with mass groups of consumers. There is, however, some debate about the ways in which mass communication actually operates. Other models have been advanced to account for the ways in which information is disseminated. This can be represented in various ways.

Single-step Communication

This early model proposed simply that a message was encoded by the sender and then interpreted individually by the mass audience.

Although superficially plausible, a little thought suggests that this is inaccurate. It assumes that the receivers constitute a passive and receptive 'mass' of individuals who do not interact with each other, but merely 'take in' information. Research has shown that reception of messages is an *active* process of interpretation, involving selective and frequently partial and heavily distorted reception of

Figure 2.3: Two-step Communication

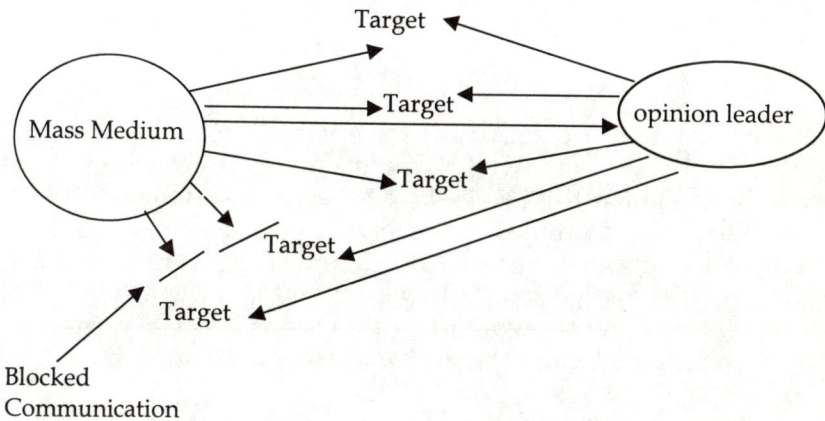

communication messages. Also people do, of course, talk to each other and thereby create influence processes affecting the way messages are received and interpreted.

Two-step Communication

Two-step communication tries to incorporate the idea of interaction and, consequentially, influence in the way in which messages are received and interpreted.

Figure 2.4: Multi-step Flows in Communication

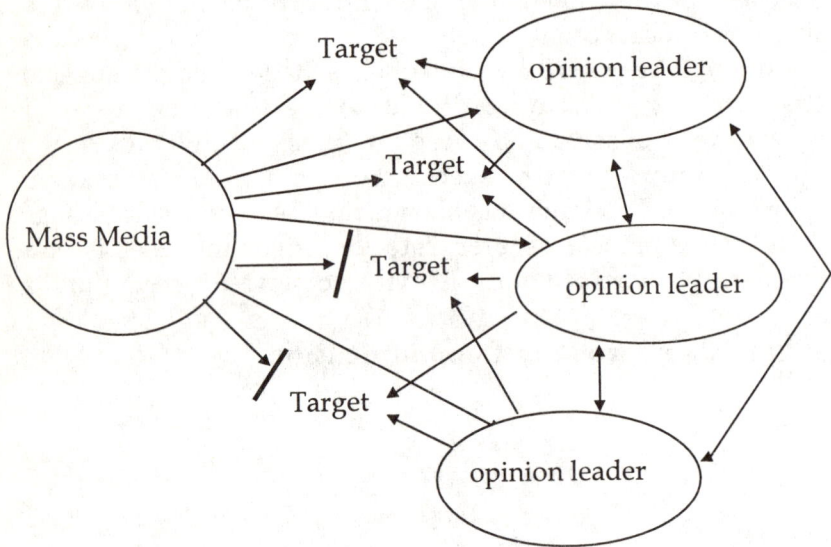

Opinion leaders, in this view, form a medium to 'filter' and disseminate the message. In research studies, such leaders have been shown to be very heavy users of the media. This, obviously, tries to make the receivers of messages an active part of the communication process and is, to some extent, a more satisfactory account. However this also opens up the possibility for more complex interactions, which a simple 'two- step' model cannot accommodate satisfactorily.

Multi-step Communication

This takes the process one step further and assumes that opinion leaders also influence each other. Research has also shown that opinion leadership in relation to consumer matters is very widespread and that these are not a very small and restricted group.

A further refinement of this idea incorporates the idea of process, and particularly feedback, into communication models. This is an attempt to deal with the complex, multi-faceted, multi-step and multi-directional nature of the communication process. This involves taking into account the fact that:

- groups have complex structures (roles, norms, leaders, attitudes, etc.);
- the perception process is structured by individual psychology, group influence and cultural factors;
- individuals interact constantly in the process of interpreting messages;
- a number of different influence processes are involved.

This produces a more complex notion of multi-step com-munication.

Figure 2.5: Multi-step Flows in Communication (2)

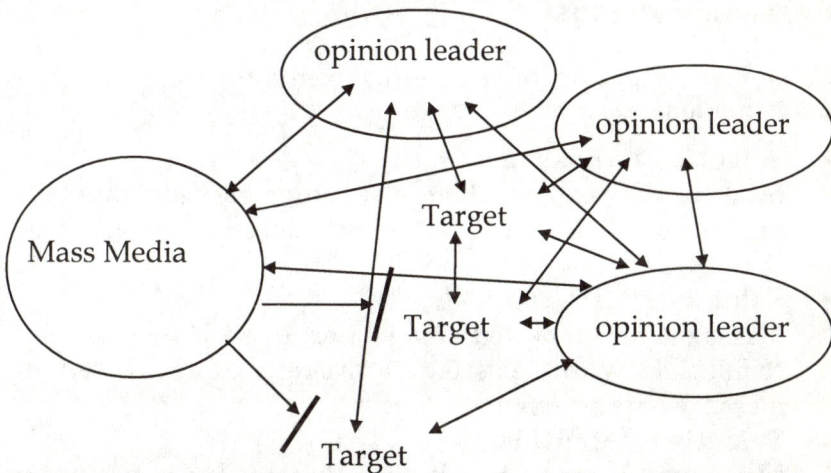

Communication problems then, arise from a number of areas and marketing communication is most concerned to overcome their effect. The main problems include:

- **noise and filtering**: as we have seen, the active and situated nature of communications processes inevitably means that they are subject to distortion from a whole range of 'countervailing factors';

- **complexity and the number of messages**: shown most graphically in the conventional attitude to 'junk mail' (the name consumers have for what marketing communicators call 'direct marketing'). The main problem faced by those using this method of communication with consumers is the fact that many people simply 'filter' it out by throwing it away without opening it or turning off advertising simply because it is intrusively obvious. This is part of a defence mechanism. It has been argued that our society is moving into an 'information overload' and that consumers are actively seeking ways in which this problem can be minimised. This often means that it is more difficult to get any attention whatsoever for advertising or promotional messages.

Activities to safeguard consumers from unwanted messages are now being pursued actively (e.g. some consumer groups are pressurising governments to safeguard their rights to avoid receiving unsolicited promotional messages).

Research Findings

Consumer reception of marketing communication has the following features.

- **Selective Exposure**
  Most people expose themselves to messages that are compatible with their existing attitudes and avoid those that are not.
- **Selective Perception**
  Messages are distorted or misinterpreted if they are not compatible with existing attitudes. More dissonant messages are rejected.
- **Selective Retention**
  Messages at variance with people's attitudes are more quickly forgotten.

Successful messages, in terms of these research findings:

- match existing attitudes;
- don't challenge ideas important to the individual.

Note how these findings undermine the popular idea of advertising and promotional effects. The idea, popularised by writers such as Vance Packard that consumers can be influenced by 'hidden persuaders' or have their minds 'bent' so that they buy products they do not really need or want, is certainly not supported by these kinds of research findings.

> *We shall now turn to the kinds of tools and techniques actually used in marketing communications practice in order to pursue marketing objectives. We shall also look briefly at the kinds of objectives pursued and, once again, how far these are from popular notions.*

Marketing Communications Tools

Corporate Image and the Control of Communications

Successful brands have a strong identity and identity is a feature of *corporate image*. Familiar brands have built up a popular image, but this has been achieved by massive investment to give companies market power or leverage. As one world leader in the business community said:

> *I have always believed that the company name is the life of an enterprise; it carries responsibility and guarantees the quality of the product..*
> *(Akio Morita, Sony Corporation)*

Corporate identity however, exists independent of corporate activity. It involves perceptions of customers, rivals, the general public and the attitudes and needs of those outside.

This image is very important for customer decisions, since one of the 'values' they are looking for in most purchases is a reliable delivery of product features. *Consumer confidence* is one of the most sought after effects of brand image and one of the expectations generated by a strong corporate image.

Making Up the Image

Factors relevant to *corporate image* include:

- commercial activities;
- products, services, prices, distribution, promotion, etc.;
- market intermediaries (i.e. trade distributors, etc.);
- suppliers (e.g. raw materials, parts, etc.);

- cultural and social environment.

We can think in terms of 'rings of corporate image', rather like the layers of an onion. The outer ring includes socio-cultural influences that affect opinions and attitudes towards industry and commerce. At the industry level, there are perceptions customers have about specific industries, while at the company level, we need to note the importance of key contacts, which will shape the way others perceive the company.

Down at brand level, there may be competing tendencies at work. For example, some brands may be better known than the parent company, especially if a 'multiple brands' strategy is being pursued. In most cases, of course, product-performance is the final arbiter of company image.

It is important to re-emphasise the significance of *corporate image control*. In over-populated and highly dynamic markets, the growing power of consumerism cannot be ignored; there are growing demands for corporate accountability and for companies to recognise their social responsibilities. As a basic aid to survival, then, there is a basic need for companies to communicate with various 'publics' and not just their customers. These would include, for example:

- consumers;
- politicians;
- employees;
- interest groups;
- investors.

Companies interested in long-term survival need to think in terms of conducting tracking studies on public opinion as a matter of course. Changes over time are, of course, inevitable and in order to formulate effective corporate strategies to counter any negative factors, information to provide the best possible basis for appropriate remedial action is essential.

Communication and *corporate development* go together. Companies also need to communicate with investors and look to the need for attracting long-term finance, to disseminate information about new products and about manufacturing techniques, as well as gather feedback from key groups about attitudes towards these areas. It has been found that, in many countries, there is strong resistance among certain groups to the use of biotechnology in food and drink production. This may consequently have a profound effect on the way in which this sector develops. Manufacturers, therefore, need to communicate with policy makers and opinion-formers, in order to:

- monitor the ways decision making is progressing in issues that will have a profound impact on the development of an industrial or service sector;
- present the most beneficial for the company or perhaps a sector as a whole.

Market research companies, such as MORI, often provide special studies of different groups (e.g. MPs, business and financial journalists, trade editors, industrialists, trade union leaders, etc.) in order to assist companies in this activity.

Companies also need to communicate with staff and recruits. High quality staff are an essential component for company success. Modern managerial theories emphasise the critical importance of attracting and retaining high quality, highly motivated and highly trained people. This can only be achieved through having an effective system for communication to keep everyone informed and, consequently, involved in the way the company develops over time.

Controlling Corporate Image

Images and symbols represent companies. Establishing a powerful and memorable image is a way of accomplishing instant, sure recognition. This also functions to convey corporate qualities and to establish a set of attributes or personality in the mind of the consumer. This is established over time and can be a powerful asset for the company.

Logos, brand names and design features of the brand do change over time, however, and it is one of the challenges facing those concerned with marketing communication to recognise the nature of the problems posed by these necessary changes. Often this reflects changes in the political and cultural environment in which the company is operating. BP, for example, has been forced to confront the problems raised for its operations by environmental activists who have raised public concerns over their operating procedures. It was recognised that failure to deal with general public concern over the safety of disposing of an oil rig in the sea would damage sales of its products and, perhaps, precipitate governmental action in terms of legislation, so appropriate measures were taken. The company now makes this a priority.

Prudential Assurance has now moved its advertising message from 'safety' to 'wisdom' to reflect changed public values.

Globalisation is likely to make control over corporate image even more important in the future. Decisions in consumer choice processes are focused more and more on dimensions of the company activities, such as social responsibility or involvement in the life of a country or region, and away from direct comparisons in terms of product features.

Research and corporate image monitoring are essential to check effectiveness. The costs of image making are high and it needs to be established that the resources invested in this process are achieving the aims required. There is, above all, a need for effective policies if the company is to communicate with various 'publics', which are important to its development. Consequently, there is also a need for reliable indicators of corporate image. MORI has developed a series of scales for image characteristics, using them to monitor change (or the effects of campaigns).

Companies are also involved in periodically 'repositioning' themselves to fit in with the changes occurring naturally in the market – whether this involves consumer tastes, competitor activity or technological change. Repositioning refers to the way image characteristics can be represented on a matrix based on consumer perceptions of the company and its competitors.

It is worth noting the differential importance of corporate image in various parts of the world. Whereas, for companies in the USA or mainland Europe, spending on promoting corporate image to the general public, or to political parties or interest groups, is regarded as important, most UK companies spend little on anyone but their customers. Industrial manufacturers and pharmaceutical manufacturers, on the other hand, see governmental and industrial investors as much more important, and spending levels are much higher in this area of corporate image making.

Figure 2.6: Image Map of US Automobile Makers and their Products (after John Koten, "Car Makers Use Image Map as Tool to Position Products" *Wall Street Journal* 22 March 1984)

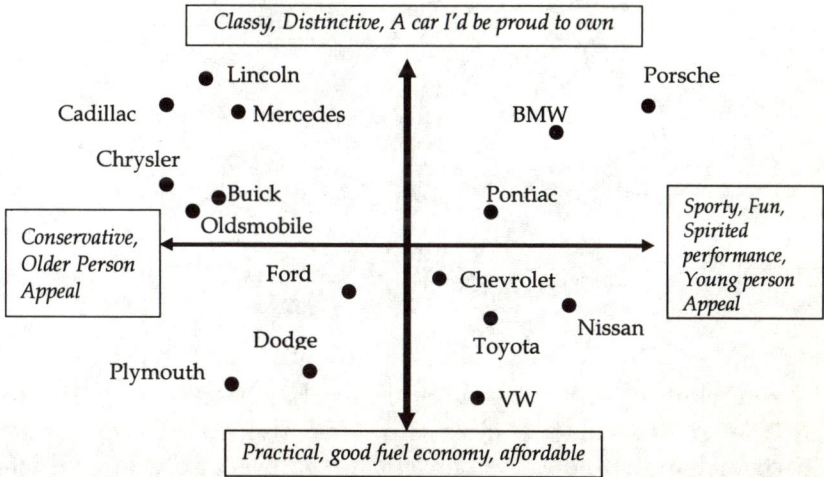

Classy, Distinctive, A car I'd be proud to own

● Lincoln   Porsche

Cadillac ●   ● Mercedes   BMW   ●

Chrysler   ●

●Buick   Pontiac
● Oldsmobile   ●

Conservative, Older Person Appeal   Sporty, Fun, Spirited performance, Young person Appeal

Ford   ● Chevrolet
●   ●
Dodge   ● Nissan
Plymouth ●   Toyota
●   ● VW

Practical, good fuel economy, affordable

NO MORE HEROES

The market for guitars and amplifiers has been badly affected by the growth of the microchip and the rise of specialist keyboard instruments which can be sold cheaply but which offer a huge range of effects and features and appeal to everyone from the novice to the virtuoso.

Guitars require some basic skills before they can even be played and tend also to be thought of as more 'masculine' than keyboards, although that prejudice is slowly being broken down.

Rockfem is a new company marketing an electric guitar for the female player and has developed an exciting portfolio of products designed to appeal to female players of all styles and in every age group. Many of the special features relate to the construction and mechanics of the instrument. Ranges have been extended to include slimmer necks and short-scale fretboards for smaller hands, light yet responsive and accurate strings, sensitive machine heads and new, user-friendly effects controls offering visual cues to the sounds being produced. Microelectronics on board makes it possible to offer pre-set ranges of sound effects.

Although this addresses a real need amongst novice players in general, market research shows that the problem of acquiring the knowledge to make the kinds of sounds you want is more acute amongst female players. They generally lack the contact with other players of their own age which male novices develop very quickly. At the same time, this is intended as a serious, technical development that will, the company believes, also be a great benefit to players at every level, because of the speed and convenience it affords during performance.

Research has shown that one of the problems for companies wishing to sell their instruments to women is the lack of suitable role models for female players. The company hopes to recruit a range of suitable sponsors for the products involved from the burgeoning female rock scene but also from notable female jazz players, classical musicians and from the folk music scene.

2.1 *What are the communication problems facing the marketing manager of Rockfem?*

2.2 *Describe the targets for marketing communications by the company. Suggest the most appropriate media for each group. Identify the key problems.*

2.3 *Draw up a practical programme for communicating with the target groups. What kinds of influence are likely to be most effective for this programme?*

2.4 *Identify the main obstacles to effective communication with this audience. Suggest possible remedies.*

2.5. *Draw diagrams to illustrate the ways influence is assumed to operate with this kind of group. Identify what you suspect may be important factors in making this kind of group less subject to such influence.*

2.6 *What, in your opinion, are the effects of opinion leadership likely to be in the marketing of these instruments?*

3
ADVERTISING

Advertising is a form of commercial promotion of products, services, institutions, ideas or persons that aims to recommend that buyers purchase particular items or to influence relevant attitudes or behaviour. It aims:

- to make buyers aware of a product/brand;
- to make buyers like a product/brand;
- to persuade buyers to purchase a product/brand.

It has also been described as "the mass communication of a promise"(i.e. it promises the gratification of some want or the satisfaction of some need). Advertising, it might be said, *translates* a product into the capacity to satisfy buyers' wants.

Advertising strategy is not an autonomous element. It is part of marketing strategy. Marketing strategy, in its turn, is part of corporate strategy. Commonly, advertising strategies are themselves part of a broader marketing communication strategy, which includes a variety of different marketing communication tools.

How Advertising Works and Where it 'Fits In'

Advertising seeks to influence what consumers 'do'. This is not to say, however, that advertising seeks simply 'to make consumers buy'. The basic theory relating consumer behaviour to advertising and promotion assumes that there are 'psychological steps' to a product being bought. This approach is called a 'hierarchy of effects' model.

It is argued that advertising seeks to gain, in order of sequence, the following from the consumer.

1. *Attention* of targeted consumers.
2. *Interest* of consumers, working with the principle that there is 'selectivity' of perception.
3. *Desire* of consumers, by 'engineering' appeals to meet their identified needs.
4. *Conviction of consumers* using 'closing techniques', which make the decision and the purchase process easier.
5. *Action* of consumers, which can be seen as the outcome of a process rather than simply the result of advertising.

Types of Media

Media are the vehicles through which advertising messages are disseminated. The main types of media employed in advertising are:

- newspapers;
- magazines;
- television;
- film;
- radio;
- outdoors (posters);
- transit (bus slogans, car cards).

New media are being developed which combine some of the features of the old, e.g. video cassettes and computer games are now important vehicles for advertising. The internet also seems set to become an ever more powerful and important avenue for advertising a wider and wider range of products and services.

We all believe we can recognise advertising when we see it. It involves many different styles, however, and given the range of media used, we need to think carefully to see its nature. The main features of advertising are that it is:

- **mass communication**: rather than person to person;
- **commercial communication**: media charge for it;
- **speedy communication**: it can reach large numbers of people quickly;
- **sponsored communication**: sellers put their name/company's name to messages.

The information conveyed in advertising content reflects the sellers' interest. The contents of advertisements are controlled by the seller and this is used as a means of persuasion, to influence the attitudes of potential buyers, users or other relevant groups or individuals with whom the advertiser seeks to communicate.

There are a number of different groups involved in advertising.

- **Advertisers**: i.e. those who sponsor the messages communicated;
- **Buyers**: who purchase the means by which the advertising is broadcast;
- **Media**: carrying the messages;
- **Advertising agencies**: which produce the advertisements and translate the message of the advertiser into the form it takes in the medium used.

In order to get the message across, various methods of communication are open to the communicator. These include:

- media advertising;
- public relations;
- selling;
- merchandising (point-of-purchase promotion);
- packaging.

All of these can be regarded as varieties of advertising. In this section we shall deal with media advertising and consider some of the others later in this book. The various objectives of media advertising may be pursued including:

- making an immediate sale;
- informing the market about availability;
- developing primary demand;
- introducing special terms;
- branding awareness/build brand loyalty;
- increasing market share;
- increasing frequency of use;
- encouraging distributors to stock and sell;
- promoting new uses;
- creating corporate image;
- announcing new servicing arrangements.

Plans for Marketing Communications

Marketing communications may be on a person to person basis or on a mass scale depending on the objectives being pursued and the nature of the market. Advertising is only part of the communications 'mix' and its effects are limited by psychological, cultural and social factors, so that, taken by itself, it rarely results in sales.

Various stages are involved in the execution of a communications strategy. It is necessary to define target groups and to investigate the purchase and decision making processes involved in their consumer behaviour. We then need to define their information needs, which will enable us to determine the nature of appeals likely to be effective. Then we can define communication objectives and, on that basis, allocate communication tasks to tactical resource areas (e.g. selling, advertising). Obviously this requires that the budget available to us is estimated and that communication tasks are allocated between marketer and distribution channels. These should be harmonised for maximum effect.

It is essential to integrate promotional strategy into marketing strategy. This necessitates developing models of promotional effects in order to assess how they can be employed in the achievement of marketing objectives. *Advertising message strategies*, of which there are a number of different types, are the means by which these objectives are to be realised. *Content strategies* are based on research. This research aims to answer the question of what consumers consider important (e.g. ease of preparation, flavour, colour, nutritive value, etc.).

There are two possibilities in relation to attribute selection: a consumer-oriented approach or a product-oriented approach. A *consumer-oriented approach* will start with the idea that advertising and promotional activity needs to be directed towards the identified needs of the consumer. A *product-oriented approach*, which is much more 'traditional', begins with the idea that the company has 'products' that it needs to sell and it is necessary to present them in the best possible light.

The consumer-oriented approach (also called the *marketing concept*) insists that successful products are those that meet consumer needs. The product-oriented approach involves persuading consumers that they have a need for the product.

The messages, which are sent out aim to accomplish these aims, but there are a number of factors influencing the actual effects which these messages have.

- **Source credibility**: Who is the source of the message? What is their interest? Are they biased? How reliable is the information they are providing? Can we believe what they say?
- **Strength of the claim**: Is it believable? Is it credible? Is it reasonable?

Most research evidence suggests moderate levels of discrepancy between existing beliefs and message claims are likely to maximise the degree of persuasion. This is because new information needs to be assimilated into an existing world view, with a set of firmly established attitudes and beliefs. If this picture is threatened or undermined by new information, major adjustment is needed and individuals tend to resist the need to do this as much as they can seek instead to retain balance in the cognitive system.

One of the most powerful types of appeal, which hinges on the importance of maintaining balance and an initial reaction to dynamic change, is the *social threat* appeal. This rests on the consumer's tendency towards conformity with social norms, which is present, to a greater or lesser degree, in all human beings. The feeling that 'everyone is doing it' can be a powerful incentive for many people, while, at the least, the idea that this is a widespread practice will reduce our resistance to the idea of buying a product, since this means that it must be generally socially acceptable.

Using *humour* in the message can also be exceptionally effective. This is particularly true nowadays when advertising is expected to be entertaining and engaging simply to get the attention of the customer for a very short length of time, so that well-told jokes, carefully constructed so that the viewer derives pleasure from repeated viewing, have become a staple format for the delivery of advertising messages.

Fear appeals are somewhat controversial. Fear is widespread in our society, and whole industries (e.g. insurance or the sale of health foods) are founded on anxieties. We live, it is said in a 'risk society', surrounded by all manner of threats to our environment and we have approach/avoidance reflexes built into our basic behaviour. Abraham Maslow argued for the importance of 'safety needs' as the most basic aspect of human motivation. Are appeals based on fear, therefore, powerful and effective? Apparently not.

There are problems with fear appeals. First, the complexity of anxiety as a psychological state. Janis and Feshbach in a study of dental hygiene, exposed groups to messages with different degrees of fear appeal. They found strong fear appeals less effective and that a 'boomerang' hostility reaction was created in the minds of those exposed.

Anti-smoking fear appeals were found to be most effective with low-anxiety individuals, with high esteem and a high ability to face problems on topics of low personal significance.

There are various ways of dealing with fear. The three psycho-dramas theory proposed that these involve responses where, first, unwelcome information is either denied or attenuated, second consumers believe, "I am the exception to the rule" (personal optimism) or, in the third option, there is a 'magical defusing process'.

Fear responses are not uniform, but vary according to the situation, the topic and the person. A US study of insurance marketing found that high-fear messages are more likely to motivate 'older liberals' and older blue-collar black people, but not others. Fear appeals can only be effective in highly segmented markets.

Comparative advertising is also controversial. 'Knocking copy' as it is sometimes called, is much more common nowadays. This advertising draws attention to failures of competitive products or enumerates the superior characteristics of the advertiser's brand. Its use may be related to more open, competitive markets or the rise of consumer movements and consumer rights issues. The effectiveness of such campaigns is disputed however.

One-sided Versus Two-sided Presentations

One of the commonest views of advertising is that is lacks credibility because it is biased and presents a distorted version of 'the facts'. Does this mean that a more balanced viewpoint will prove more believable?

Hovland researched this in connection with US army training and indoctrination films in World War II and found that the degree and direction of change differed according to the original opinions expressed by individuals. One-sided presentation proved more effective for producing a congruent change. There was also an educational factor, the better educated amongst the subjects were less influenced by the one-sided appeals.

Etgar and Goodwin, in a study of advertising effects found that two-sided presentations "yielded significantly higher attitudes towards new brand introduction than one-sided [presentations]". This was influenced by 'inoculation or immunisation theory'. In this approach, small amounts of unfavourable information were introduced into advertisements, on the assumption that this would produce 'protection' from competitors' attacks. The danger here is consumers not finding solutions to problems, but simply more problems of choosing!

There are, however, a number of critical issues arising in relation to advertising, and formulating an advertising campaign involves far more than developing a neat story line with a good joke or perhaps a 'fear' appeal. If the campaign is to influence the target group, how often must advertising be used? What media must be employed? How do these different media influence the target? Does repetition, always assumed to be an essential weapon in the psychology of advertising, have a positive or negative affect on consumers? Does the context of communication have a bearing on the effectiveness of the advertising? What about the source of the message? How does morality, for example, influence the way in which advertising messages are perceived?

All of these credibility factors can strongly affect the

success or failure of a campaign. It is important to recognise that careful planning, use of research and testing at all stages are vital prerequisites for effective campaigns.

Creative Strategy and Tactics

Basic advertising strategy derives from the marketing plan. This will involve a creative implementation section in which the objectives of the marketing plan are broken down into elements that can be related to the practical content, format and mode of delivery for the communications involved in the advertising/promotional strategy.

The advertising plan also contains a *creative strategy rationale*. This summarises the thinking behind an advertising campaign and translates the strategy statement in the marketing plan into terms appropriate for a creative team. For example, it will contain a statement of the attributes to be stressed, the benefits which the product promises to deliver to the consumer, and so on. The characteristics of the target group are carefully detailed, since this will provide a key basis for the way the advertising can be developed (indicating, as it does, the kinds of people involved, how they live, what is important to them, what media they are exposed to, etc.).

A clear statement, detailing all these factors provides a reference point and ensures consistency of effort amongst all the groups and individuals working on different dimensions of the marketing communications programme.

A copy platform, which is concerned with the implementation of the creative strategy, will also be needed. This is a document providing the basis for the messages to be used in the advertising. The principal elements in a copy platform are:

- principal theme or 'selling idea';
- the 'mood' of ads;
- the expression of product features.

Clearly, advertising may be more or less successful depending on the conditions in the setting. For example, bad weather will have a considerable impact on the sales of particular sorts of goods and the advertising messages relating, for example, to central heating systems or foreign holidays in the sun, will be much more friendly and positive. Conditions favourable to advertising in general relate to a range of factors.

The *utility* offered by goods is a key element. When goods

provide satisfaction(s), which cannot be matched by competitive products, and fully support the claims made by appropriate advertising, then this 'reputational' dimension creates a very favourable climate in which advertising can take place.

The *appropriateness* of different elements of the marketing mix is also important.

Brand names that are appealing and fitting for the product make advertising easier. So does good packaging, which matches the kinds of messages involved in the advertising.

Pricing should reflect the kinds of claims the product is making and fit both the use intended for the product and the profile of the intended user.

It is essential that *differentiation* and *competitive advantage* are carried through. A product which is distinctive, and which makes substantive claims to deliver satisfactions to mark it off from competitors, will certainly make advertising much easier.

Strong primary demand is always an important advantage for the advertiser and may shape the kinds of messages involved in the advertising campaign. The same is true for *big* or *expanding markets*. The demand coming from the customer in these circumstances shapes, to a very large degree, the role advertising can, and should, play.

In order to meet these needs, however, it is essential the systems in place can ensure that customers not only get the goods but are also supported and maintained in the best possible manner. A good *distribution system* and good *working relations with retailers* are the key to success here. The value of this can be seen, for instance, in the success of Compaq within the personal computer market, which has been built on close attention to the important role of the distribution system and the retailer in liaison with the customer in delivering the quality and reliability Compaq has claimed in their advertising and they have insisted on premium prices to deliver it. Much of this has gone in excellent margins for its retailers, however, while at the same time, the company has insisted on maintaining the very highest standards of service and customer satisfaction from those involved.

A *strong emotional motivation* towards a product (e.g. concerns about the safety of food following a medical report or an outbreak of disease) will create a very favourable climate towards advertising which promises protection.

Finally, of course, it is extremely important that, within the company itself, there should be a *favourable management attitude* towards advertising. What resources are dedicated to the process depend on management attitudes and success depends, at least in part, on the commitment management displays towards it.

Advertising in the Marketing Mix

Promotion, in a real sense, involves buying patronage. Apart from the costs involved in advertising, enterprises are prepared to take on the costs of stores, salesmen, price cuts and the provision of special services to customers in order to get goods sold.

Why use advertising? It is sometimes argued, by those who see advertising as potentially dangerous or socially corrosive, that we should encourage choice based only on the virtues of the goods themselves.

Advertising, however, serves good economic and practical purposes. It is used because it increases profit by pre-selling and because offering messages and information about a product assists in the choice process. This, then, reduces the costs of personal selling, since it removes from the point-of-sale much of the process of providing information about a product.

It also serves a number of important functions in the long-term history of the enterprise. Defensive advertising, for instance, aims to protect the place of a company within the marketplace and to resist, for example, negative messages or mistaken beliefS on the part of consumers. It also 'smoothes out' fluctuations in demand by stimulating the market when it is sluggish.

Advertising is not just concerned with persuasion or 'manipulation'. Buyers are active users of information, rather than simply passive recipients. When we look at how buyers use advertising, it is clear that many purposes are being served.

It is used *for information*, as a source of technical data about how to use a product, about how to get a product and about what kinds of satisfactions a product can provide, as an aid to the imagination.

It is used also *to protect or enhance the self-image of consumers*. It provides the consumer with meanings and reasons to buy a product and, in a sense, a vocabulary of motives in the use and enjoyment of a product.

Advertising Appeals

Research has shown that there are a number of 'psychological steps' to a sale. These are affecting the consumer's:

- attention;
- interest;
- desire;
- conviction;
- action.

The objectives of advertising must take account of these steps. At each stage, advertising must accomplish certain behavioural objectives, but these must be seen as part of an overall set of corporate and marketing aims for the enterprise – getting the attention of new consumers, developing their interest and awakening their desire involve creative strategy – but the ultimate aim will be to increase profits by increasing sales volume. This is usually accomplished by means of attempts to affect demand. Choice needs to be made between three pairs of goals, the communications strategist must aim to:

- stimulate either primary demand or selective demand;
- promote either the brand ('brand image') or the firm selling it ('corporate image');
- cause either indirect or direct action.

Primary demand is concerned with the generic product/service. There might, for instance, be a need to promote consumption of 'fish' or 'computers' where there is little or no branding involved. This might be where, for example, there is monopoly control or state ownership or where a product is new and there is limited knowledge of what products are or how they can be used.

The promotion of *selective demand* is more usual. This involves the promotion of a particular brand by:

- increasing use by present users;
- increasing numbers of users;
- promoting new uses.

This may be accomplished by a number of different strategies. *Brand image promotion* involves developing a product concept so that the personality or image of the *product* matches the needs of the consumer.

Promotion relating to the *corporate image* involves develop-ing a patronage concept in which the company behind the goods or services becomes the basis, for example, for consumer confidence in the safety or quality of the product in question. This may be used where the product portfolio of the company is diverse and it may be inappropriate to emphasise those product characteristics that cannot be generalised or transferred to other products within the portfolio.

The connection to, and the differences between, these twin aspects of promotional activity are apparent if we examine their nature more closely.

Brand Image

The determinants of brand image are various. The *corporate image* of the enterprise can be a very important factor in itself. Is it, for example, a caring enterprise or has it earned a reputation for bad practice in labour relations or care for the environment?

The *consumers* of the product themselves imbue the product with a particular image. Is it an 'exclusive' or a 'mass market' product? How old are those who use the product? Are they perceived to be a particular 'type' of person?

Store image, or the *retailers* who sell the product, also lends it important aspects of its appeal. For example, products only available in prestigious or high status stores will transfer some of these qualities to the product itself. Both manufacturers and retailers are concerned to protect their appeal from damage able to be imparted from either side. If a store or a product has a particular reputation, an inappropriate pairing may cause damage.

The *physical features* of the product can also be important. Consumers evaluate the quality and appeal of a product, in many cases, by the way in which it appears. For example, in the case of packaging or product design, these often provide primary cues for the potential purchaser about the quality, freshness, status, intended usage, etc. of the product.

While promotion and advertising promise certain things, success depends on the 'truth' upon which these are based. The *satisfaction* customers actually get from the product is the acid test. Marketing, as has been said, is about selling "goods that don't come back to customers who do". If satisfaction is not delivered, then the customer is unlikely to make a repeat purchase and, apart from certain kinds of unscrupulous enterprises, most companies are trying to build up business over the longer term. Repeat purchase, and its by-product customer recommendation, are, of course, extremely important.

Marketing communications in general, and *advertising* in

particular, aims to provide the basis for brand image to be developed and sustained. It attempts to control and regulate the messages consumers are receiving about the brand, but before all else, it needs to find out what the messages should be and how it should relate to the needs of the consumer.

Corporate Image

The purposes of corporate image are more wide-ranging than the purposes of the brand image. Companies seek to operate profitably and to succeed in their corporate mission. This may not necessarily relate to the success or long-term existence of a particular product or brand. One of the first things an enter-prise has to do, and must periodically reconsider, involves asking the question, "What business are we in?" Being tied to a product, a technology or a production process, made obsolete by changing technology or consumer tastes will be fatal for a company unless it focuses on deeper issues and addresses customer needs, rather than the products it has made in the past. Corporate aims, then, are focused on survival and prosperity in the wider world.

One of the most important and fundamental objectives able to be pursued with this in mind is the objective *to make friends*. Building corporate image means having various sorts of 'publics' – not just consumers, but a whole range of other groups which are identified as important for the image of the company and its relations with its operating environment – persuaded of the value and virtue of the corporate entity and its operations.

A key objective, therefore, is *to build confidence and goodwill* among groups who are important to the company. This may be accomplished through advertising, but also through other sorts of corporate activity, such as sponsorship.

This often aims *to raise a firm's prestige* – association with and promotion of 'cutting-edge' research, participation in business initiatives, endorsement by prestigious public bodies or notable individuals will accomplish this. It is then vital that this is made public. Marketing communications through advertising and publicity will then seek *to publicise the firm's prestige* by, for example, advertising the successes the company has achieved in commercial terms, any awards it has been given or what acknowledgement there has been by, say, government or key public institutions.

The objective *to publicise the firm's strengths* may be

undertaken with slightly different aims in mind. When issues of quality or competence are of concern (among the consumers, the general public or the investors in a company) it may be important to advertise the strengths of the management team, the achievements of the research division or the performance of the sales team.

Advertising then, is concerned with producing direct or indirect action on the part of the consumer. Some advertising (e.g. small ads in newspapers) intends to cause those reading the ad to respond directly by sending off a coupon or telephoning to order a product. Other advertising (e.g. the corporate image advertising we have just mentioned) does not try to provoke a direct and immediate response. It seeks rather to influence the way decisions are taken in the future, to shape the ways in which consumers regard or perceive a company, its activities or its products.

Clearly, advertising is not all of a piece, but falls into many different categories or types. We need to consider some of the ways we can describe these various types and some of the reasons for their diversity.

Classifying Advertising

Advertising can be looked at from the point of view of the buyer or the seller. If we consider advertising by type of buyer it can be seen as directed towards five main types.

1. **Ultimate consumers**

   This covers advertising directed at those who consume a product and is a vital, but not the only, source of demand. In families, for example, the ultimate consumers of food are the family members, including perhaps very young children, but food is bought, for the most part by adults who usually take children's demands into account, but are also considering, for example, financial or health factors. These 'gatekeepers' must, of course, also be taken into account. The level of satisfaction involved is relevant; those who actually eat food are said to be deriving 'primary satisfaction', whereas a housewife buying for her family will derive 'secondary satisfaction' from their enjoyment of the food.

2. **Middlemen**

   These are intermediaries in the channels between the producer and the consumer of a product. They would include retailers, salesmen, wholesalers, franchisees, etc. Advertising to these groups will obviously be concerned with persuading them of the wisdom in dealing with the products or services and of the best ways they can deal with and provide information to the customers. It often aims to harmonise the promotional efforts going on in various parts of the channel with the messages being put out by the manufacturer.

3. **Purchasing agents**

These act on behalf of retailers or groups of industrial producers buying-in goods for their enterprises. Advertising directed at them emphasises specific issues related to the nature of their place in the market.

4. **Organisational buyers**

These buyers are purchasing as part of their business (e.g. buying-in office supplies). Organisational buying is more complex and often involves groups and individuals within organisations, rather than single buyers, in a decision process. These stakeholders may all have different priorities, different levels of involvement and different degrees of power to exercise. Advertising directed at them may well be channelled through specialist journals, be displayed at specialist locations (e.g. exhibitions, shows or conferences) and be concerned with technical and commercial aspects of product usage.

5. **Advisors/Buying influences**

Particular groups (e.g. consultants or leading experts) will be particularly influential in shaping the kinds of decisions taken by non-specialists. There are also individuals who function as 'opinion leaders' within the population at large in all aspects of consumer behaviour. When new products are being launched, or existing products modified, it is particularly important that these 'influentials' should be informed and preferably have had the opportunity to try the products in question. At this early stage of the product life cycle, particular efforts are made to identify and communicate with these groups and individuals, with disproportionate investment in advertising and promotion. The calculation is made that endorsement and recommendation by these people will have a very significant impact on the rest of the population. The information they have been given, and their experience of product usage, is translated into influence over much larger sections of the population, assuming a 'trickle down' effect with a high degree of lateral, rather than just vertical and direct communication going on.

If we consider advertising by type of seller, then this indicates the kind of objectives it is likely to be pursuing.

Advertisements for Whom?

All but a small proportion of the mass communications media, so important in modern life, also function to disseminate advertising messages. Even when a broadcast medium is specifically reserved for non-commercial messages, it still carries advertising or promotional communications (e.g. political broadcasting or 'public service' messages to promote safe behaviour or encourage desirable attitudes).

The main commercial sources for advertising and promotional messages, however, come from the following areas.

1.   **Manufacturers**

These are, in the main, likely to be aimed at consumers in the general population. The nature of the advertising will depend on the product. This will go all the way from highly specialised industrial goods and services, supplied to business organisations, to fast-moving consumer goods (FMCGs) in huge markets dispersed over immense geographical areas.

2.   **Retailers**

Stores also advertise. They aim to promote themselves and, as part of that, they also promote the products they sell. The advertising is therefore serving various purposes. The 'store image' is being promoted and this is at least partly derived from the kinds of goods it makes available. It may also focus on key factors, such as service and guarantees of quality. Each retailer will have a very clear idea of the customer profile towards which this advertising is directed. Most often, this will be based on market research. This research may involve formal fact gathering and analysis involving a specialist agency or simply a more or less systematic monitoring of the kinds of information gathered by most firms in the course of their business, such as sales returns, customer feedback and sales personnel information. Increasingly ubiquitous information technology means that more and more non-specialists are able to manipulate information which they have stored or access databases which can tell them who their customers are and what sorts of messages are likely to be effective in reaching them.

3. **Sellers of services**

Marketing services faces quite specific problems. Each service will have a specific bundle of satisfactions it will aim to deliver to the customer. Unlike the advertising and marketing of goods, there is no tangible item involved in the transaction between buyer and seller. Advertising, consequently, focuses on the experience and rewards offered by the seller of the service. Customer satisfaction is paramount and a lot of service advertising involves endorsements from satisfied customers, along with explanations of the systems used to ensure the delivery of high levels of service and customer care.

4. **Generic product groups**

In advertising for these groups, the aim is to encourage levels of usage of the product type, rather than the brand. This type of advertising is use in marketing 'basic', unbranded products more or less direct from producer. Agricultural and horticultural products (e.g. eggs, apples, potatoes, meat or fresh fish) are often advertised in this way. Producers may not be able to market effectively as individuals but pay a levy to an organisation or marketing board, which then commissions advertising of the product type.

5. **Non-profit organisations**

Advertising for charities, aid organisations, such as Oxfam, or non-profit making bodies, such as the Boy Scouts, Mind, Scope or Greenpeace, is particularly important, since their main purpose is fundraising in order to carry out important work on behalf of needy groups. At the same time, their advertising may need to serve a number of different purposes – from giving information about the work of the organisation to indicating how donations are used and how donations can be sent in or arranged. Unlike other kinds of advertising, non-profit bodies do not usually claim to be offering a product or service to meet the needs of the target group. Rather, they are providing for the needs of other groups and are requiring funding from the target group for goods and services that this group will not receive. Some organisations have claimed that recently there have been such demands on the goodwill of these target groups that many are now suffering from 'compassion fatigue' and are refusing to donate.

6.   **Individuals**

Most individuals who advertise themselves are either politicians, celebrities or, on a more mundane level, those who advertise their services in the 'situations wanted' columns of newspapers and magazines. Increasingly, this kind of advertising of individuals is moving into the world outside of politics. Businessmen have been involved in semi-political campaigns pursuing a single issue or have used advertising to attack others or defend themselves.

Advertising Strategy and Tactics

These must harmonise with the basic objectives of the market-ing plan. In fact, the advertising strategy is always derived from the overall marketing plan and is most often part of an overall marketing communications strategy.

The type of strategy depends on the marketing plan being followed. If the advertising is intended to differentiate the product or a particular brand, this will require a specific strategy. Product differentiation will need to focus on the main characteristics of the product type and so will involve primary promotion. Brand differentiation aimed at identifying those factors differentiating this brand from others within the product area, might be referred to as 'secondary promotion'.

As we have already said, advertising may pursue a number of different objectives, according to the primary thrust of the marketing plan.

Market expansion, as a marketing objective, will require targeting new consumers, increasing the volume of the product consumers use or causing consumers to switch from one product to another. On the other hand, *brand positioning* or *repositioning*, as a strategy, is concerned with perceptions of the product by consumers and is aimed firstly at changing how consumers perceive this particular brand in relation to its competitors.

Analysis of consumer needs, if properly executed, should indicate the optimum brand position. Positioning within the

Figure 3.1: Brand Positions of Beers and Lagers (UK market)

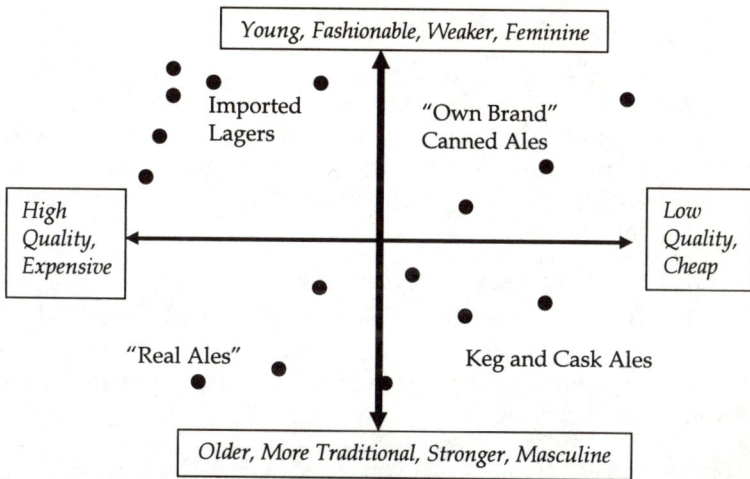

market depends entirely on what are identified by market research to be the key differentiating factors. The 'position' of the brand, relative to competitors, is ascertained by measuring consumer attitudes and behaviours. These will show, for example, which attributes of the brand (its quality image, appearance, reliability, taste or whatever) are most valued and by which kinds of customers. Behaviour, such as how a brand is used, when, by whom and how often it is purchased, will also enable the brand and its customers to be represented and compared – both to other brands and also to customer 'ideals'. These are then plotted on a two or three dimensional representation of the 'semantic space' involved.

Tactics

These strategies are pursued by means of tactics and involve the pursuit of objectives by the deployment of appropriate techniques in an organised way.

Communications objectives, being pursued in the advertising of products or services, can be thought of as involving sequential steps. Advertising would be pursuing different objectives at different stages of a campaign, according to the needs of the marketing plan.

1. **Creating awareness (of the product/brand/ characteristics)**

    Most advertising for a brand or a product starts with the need to create awareness in the mind of the consumer.

This involves developing a form of advertising that will gain the attention of the target group.

2. **Engender favourable attitudes**

    At later stages in the life cycle, the primary function of advertising is to change the way consumers feel about the product. This may not necessarily be concerned with generating purchase per se but in, for example, persuading consumers to try the product or communicating key product advantages.

3. **Generate action of purchase**

    This is, of course, the ultimate aim of all marketing of products or services; it is usually part of a process, however, and is the end result of a range of interrelated measures.

The Power of Advertising

A study of advertising in industrial markets sought to compare groups exposed to ads with those not and estimate the attitudes of these groups to competitors in order to determine how much each group bought from competing suppliers and to correlate exposure and market share.

The results indicate the reasons industrial advertising is influential with buyers. They found that advertising improves the buyer's opinion of the manufacturers and means a larger share of the market for the manufacturer. At the same time it acts as a valuable introduction for the sales force. Lack of frequency of advertising is the most common cause of programme failure. It also found that the costs of selling to groups exposed to advertising are 10 per cent to 30 per cent lower.

At the same time, non-advertiser costs of selling to groups exposed to competitor advertising were 20 per cent to 40 per cent higher. Advertising, then, increases profitability.

An advertising programme can, therefore, reduce the overall costs of selling by multiplying the effectiveness of the individual salesman far more than it increased indirect selling costs. In relation to industrial marketing, there are clear and direct benefits from advertising.

Advertising and Behaviour

In promotion, the primary means of mass communication is advertising. To evaluate its uses and limitations, we need to consider some of the behavioural aspects of advertising and bear in mind the models of influence processes put forward by consumer behaviourists, such as Katz and Lazarsfeld.

Hierarchical models of advertising are the most generally accepted. Starch (an early theorist of advertising) outlined the 'behaviour of advertising' theory.

Advertising, he argued, calls attention to, and informs people about, products and services via mass communication media. It does so by establishing a favourable or preferred association link between a need and a brand name, so that when the need arises the name will come to mind with a favourable or preferential image established.

This works, he insisted, through *repeat* advertising and through satisfactory use and performance of the product. He saw two sets of forces at work. Advertising effects were constantly weakening through fading memory and because of counter-advertising, while there was a tendency towards strengthening links through advertising repetition and the effects of experience.

The DAGMAR approach (Defining Advertising Goals for Measured Advertising Results) was developed by Colley, who argued that all commercial communications carry the prospect through four levels of understanding.

1. Unawareness to awareness.
2. Comprehension.
3. Conviction.
4. Action.

Colley saw advertising as "helping to move the consumer through one or more of these stages" towards purchase. In fact, this is very similar to Starch's model. Other hierarchical models include the 'AIDA' (Attention, Interest, Desire, Action) sequence model. This is well regarded for its simplicity and common sense appeal. The Lavidge and Steiner approach is more complex, commending awareness, knowledge, liking, preference, conviction and purchase as the stages of the process. Lavidge and Steiner relate their six steps of advertising influence to a three-phase psychological model of attitude formation. These stages are:

• cognitive (knowledge);
• affective (liking);
• cognitive (action).

Despite their plausibility, there are major problems with hierarchical models. First, they assume a sequential order, which ignores the complexity of the relationship between attitudes and behaviour. Second, they assume reciprocal relationship between attitudes and behaviour and impose a view of advertising as involving 'causality'. This is highly questionable. The tendency to use physical metaphors in relation to advertising encourages this notion of 'cause and effect' – advertising impact, hammering home a message, etc.

Lannon and Cooper criticise the main models because they make little allowance for the participation of the receiver of the communication in the process. Advertising is, in reality, consumed by sophisticated audiences. Consumers use advertising, rather than vice versa.

Products are given 'symbolic value' and there are real limits on the power of advertising, which can enhance, but not in itself cause, social change. Advertising cannot make a market grow unless it would anyway, i.e. the economic conditions must exist.

Advertising can create brand awareness but, according to informed observers, advertising's role is much less to create demand than to show people how to satisfy the demands they have by increasing the competition between brands in a market. Most modern business theorists see its main economic function as the lubrication of competition.

Attitudes, Consumer Behaviour and Advertising

So far, we have assumed that messages sent by the advertiser are received more or less directly and more or less intact by the consumer. In fact, this very rarely happens. Messages are received and understood in very different ways from that intended by those sending them. Advertising messages are subject to distortion through all stages of the transmission and reception process.

US studies assessing the influence of advertising used five measurable indicators, these were awareness, recognition, recall, attitude and buying predisposition. *Attitude* was found to be the most important element influenced by advertising. Campaigns were felt to be about changing attitudes but favourable attitudes do not necessarily mean purchase. Advertising affects attitudes, the report said, but:

> *...rather than assume that advertising's function is to affect sales directly or to have an effect on a level of the hierarchy, it would seem more functional to assume that advertising can maintain or shift*

attitudes with respect to salient product charac-teristics and their ratings.

Boyd et al, "An Attitudinal Framework for Advertising Strategy" *Journal of Marketing* (1972) Vol. 36.

Joyce argued that favourable attitudes towards a specific branded product may be reinforced by acceptable perform-ance and may encourage repeat buying. This also works in reverse, of course, so that repeated exposure to the perform-ance of a product may generate favourable attitudes towards that product.

The degree of change which advertising actually brings about is somewhat controversial. Cox saw that much of advertising functioned either to reinforce existing attitudes and behaviour or to stimulate/activate people who are already predisposed to act, rather than bringing about dramatically new attitudes or behaviours.

Attitudes then, clearly influence behaviour but not quite in the way it is commonly assumed. Advertising is likely to be more effective if it links selling points to the existing attitudes of target segments. Advertising may assist in developing trends in consumption before they are in full flow. Messages must, however, be congruent with existing attitudes or they will be 'screened out', 'sharpened' or 'levelled'. At the same time, advertising influences and is influenced by:

- personal factors;
- environmental factors;
- cultural norms;
- family life cycles;
- opinion, leadership, etc.;
- economic factors.

Target groups vary in the way these are concatenated. At the same time, advertising influences levels of awareness, percep-tion, evaluation, enquiry and purchase decision, although this effect diminishes over time.

Communications should, perhaps, be viewed as a transac-tional process. Both the audience and marketer give and take in some mutually acceptable pattern. An exchange of values in communication may not always be equitable, however; deception may take place, arising from subjective perceptions by audiences or even malpractice by the communicator. Lowe Watson suggests that advertising be seen:

...as part of a network of relationships, linking the buyer, the seller and the product advertised. This new emphasis on 'total communication' entails co-ordination of every aspect of the communications programme.

He sees this as exposing the fallacy of the economic rationality view of advertising. Advertising is often, he says, wasteful and inefficient, because the information it gives is selective, incomplete and exaggerated. For a long time, advertisers thought that they had established a simple, winning formula in the way that messages were communicated. Repetitive advertising, forever linked to the great psychologist JWB Watson, insisted on the importance of frequency and recency (stamping in). Repetition was designed to 'stamp in' brand messages. This is a credo involving a simple and direct link between the frequency with which messages are communicated, the number of times buyers are, as a consequence exposed to them, and the effect on sales. Would that it proved so simple!

The problem is that this credo ignores selective perception or diversity of response to the messages. Messages may provoke very different responses in different individuals and overexposure to a message may have a serious negative impact on buyer attitudes towards the message. Research also shows that as stimuli increase in intensity, the sensitivity of organisms towards them is diminished, so that, for example, louder noises, brighter colours or stronger tastes have a diminishing impact. More is not always better, sometimes, as they say, less is more. In establishing a image for quality, low levels of advertising and understated messages may be much more effective to achieve those communication objectives.

It has also been pointed out that the idea of repetitive advertising ignores the impact of personal influence and motivated aspects of memory, not just time. Learning is active, not merely accretive.

The role of repetitive advertising seems to be largely defensive in mature, more sophisticated marketing environments. Simple messages reminding and encouraging existing loyalties rather than direct and unsubtle entreaties to 'go out and buy' seem likely to be the appropriate messages for this type of approach.

AH! BOVRITE

Family Celebrates the Past and Looks Forward to More Success

Bovrite has been on the shelf in the British kitchen since before the nation of shopkeepers found itself facing the Kaiser across the trenches of Mons and the Somme, but of course gravy itself goes back long before that time. Making gravy used to be difficult and time consuming so when this familiar old product first came along it was an instant hit.

Many food manufacturers had tried to produce 'instant gravy' since the middle of the 19th century, trying various combinations of gravy salts, gravy browning and thickening agents. But nothing solved the problem, and the market for an 'all-in-one' product remained unfilled until two Edwardian housewives complained to their food manufacturer husbands.

Stockton managers Arthur Brigham and Neville Mortimer worked for Snexite Salt Supplies, which produced a large range of table condiments but who had surprisingly not yet addressed the problem of gravy salt. The story goes that Mrs Brigham scolded her husband for bringing home a surprise dinner guest because it did not allow her time to make gravy for the meal and the problem immediately roused his interest.

The problem was turned over to the analytical chemist who worked for the company who eventually came up with a formula which, when mixed with water and blended with the juices of roasting meat to produce a uniform, rich brown gravy. The problem was solved.

The product was an almost instant success. In a country where demand for convenience in the kitchen was growing fast, and new cooking aids appearing more and more, it caught on quickly and *Bovrite* became part of the English language.

The advertising of the product began in 1910, with a full page advertisement on the front page of the *Daily Sketch*. There was very little of the forms of advertising we would recognise today until *Bovrite* became part of the stock on the shelves of every grocer. Advertising became more and more visible, with colour posters all over the countryside.

The famous *Bovrite* Boys did not arrive until after the First World War. The artist Buck Francis came up with an idea, possibly inspired by the numbers of beggars on the streets in the hungry days after the War, of two ragamuffin characters smelling the gravy through an open kitchen window and breathing the famous phrase "Ahhhhhhh...*Bovrite*!!!".

The posters and characters became part of the folklore of the time. It is said by some that Chaplin's tramp character owes at least something to the interest created by these posters. Cartoonists began to draw similar characters as a long running recognition of the appeal of the characters. Norbert Giles said of the characters:

> *The strength of the characters comes from the basic but simple themes they exemplify – hunger and appetite. Everyone recognises these needs, everyone has known hunger and longing for something, whether it is fame, power or food. We talk about this in food terms – 'the sweet smell of success'. These characters represent an urge that everyone can understand.*

The cartoon has been mimicked over the years to lampoon famous politicians; Ramsay MacDonald, Hitler and Stalin and, in more recent times, Healey and Callaghan.

The *Bovrite* Boys have become part of the British psyche. The famous poster series has run virtually unchanged since the 1930s, apart from periodic 'tweaking' of the wardrobe. The company used to keep a stock of clothing at the factory to lend out to customers who wanted to impersonate the boys in fancy dress costumes.

Most recently, the company has decided to employ, for the first time, real actors to represent the *Bovrite* Boys. New actors are chosen each year, in a highly publicised competition. This has not threatened the popularity of the cartoon characters, however, who continue to represent the company on posters and in some television advertising.

The product continues to dominate, with more than 80 per cent of the gravy salt market. In spite of the decline of the formal meal, and the growth of 'snacking and grazing', the product still seems indispensable to every kitchen. This is possibly because it represents one of the first, and most familiar 'convenience products'. Housewives and their families have grown up with it and see *Bovrite* as, in some way, what 'gravy' actually means.

New product forms, such as granules, and special formulae for vegetarians − a growing sector of the market, especially amongst younger families and single people − have been hugely successful. The *Bovrite* name has also moved into the general sauce market, reflecting the growing sophistication of the consumer and the growth of highly diverse food markets. The same granule technology, introduced at the early stage of the market growth, has enabled the company to take a similarly commanding position within this market.

The company has long moved out of the original Stockton factory and is now relocated near Midtown, Cheshire. The larger facilities allow the company to cope with worldwide demand for the product from expatriates everywhere and also, surprisingly, from Belgium. Housewives there acquired the habit from troops in the trenches during World War I and Belgium is now the biggest export market for the product.

The essential 'Britishness' of the product, however, is emphasised by tales from all over the world of puzzled customs officers confronted by suitcases full of packets of mysterious brown powder, carried only by homesick 'Brits' who only want to hang on to the taste of home. The most regular long distance phone call at the *Bovrite* factory asks, "Where can we get it in this part of the world?"

3.1   *What are the main messages involved in Bovrite advertising? How are these communicated in the advertising?*

3.2   *Why has the slogan and the advertising imagery, proven so successful over a long period of time? Why has it managed to appeal to generations in different circumstances?*

3.3   *How, do you think, is the market for sauces likely to change over the next twenty years in your own country? Indicate what advertising messages and media you might employ in order to address these changes.*

3.4   *How does a company such as this communicate with customers who want 'traditional' gravy salt, and those who want 'vegetarian' products? Consider the ways in which advertising might effectively target such groups and describe the kinds of messages that might be appropriate for them.*

3.5   *Describe or draw alternative characters to act as the 'brand personality' for Bovrite products. Explain the reasons for your choice.*

4

SALES PROMOTION AND PERSONAL SELLING

Why include sales promotions and personal selling in a text concerned with 'marketing messages'? Precisely because the sales personnel, so important for these activities, are the 'messengers' of the enterprise. More than any other individuals within the business enterprise, the sales force are engaged in direct, face to face communication with clients and the messages they pass on in these interactions shape how the enterprise and its products are viewed by existing customers, 'prospects' and many publics who may be extremely important to the continuing operation of the enterprise. These activities and personnel are key components in any integrated communication strategy.

Sales Promotion

According to the Institute of Sales Marketing:

> *Sales promotion involves a range of tactical marketing techniques that fit within a strategy and are intended to add value as part of the process of achieving specific marketing objectives.*

Sales promotions may take a variety of forms in order to generate consumer interest in, or awareness of, a product and its features. Special reduced rates or free samples are one of the commonest tactics but there are many others.

Sales promotional techniques are a means for specific objectives to be best achieved (e.g. inducing trials, affecting usage behaviour, switching from one brand to another). Examples of sales promotional techniques include:

- price promotions;
- free samples;
- coupon offers (money-off offers);
- price reductions;

- competitions;
- free gifts;
- combination pack offers;
- off-price labels;
- trading stamps;
- samples;
- exhibitions and demonstrations;
- catalogues;
- on-pack offers.

'Non-media advertising' and below-the-line advertising (or activity) are alternative terms used to refer to sales promotion activities. Sales promotions is a vital tool in the repertoire of the marketing communication manager and is used extensively. Because there is often a direct link between the promotion (e.g. reduced-price bargains, free gift offers, competitions) and short-term sales volume, the use of sales promotions is seen as a key mechanism to address fluctuations in market performance.

Reasons for Using Sales Promotions as a Quick Fix

The tendency is to use sales promotions in order to address short-term difficulties in the market. This derives from a number of pressures.

- Pressure to boost sales figures. These are often attended to on a very short-term basis.
- Pressure produced by shortened product life cycles.
- Pressure caused by over populated, highly competitive, highly dynamic markets.
- The effectiveness of sales promotional techniques themselves.
- The availability of 'off-the-peg' solutions offered by 'full service' promotional agencies.

This kind of 'fire fighting' is not the only way such techniques can be used, of course.

Strategic Uses of Sales Promotional Techniques

Strategic approaches – emphasising long-term development and connections to other aspects of corporate planning – are preferred by other marketing communications theorists. This is because they permit a cumulative development of tactics (linking offers, or different kinds of promotional prog-rammes to each other) over time. There is also a synergy between different types of promotional and communicative activity and the short-term perspective does not enable this to work to the fullest extent. Single, isolated promotions do not, then, work as hard as they might if they were working together. This also means that a strategic approach is more cost-effective and, basically, saves money.

Retailer or Middleman Promotions as a 'Push' Policy

Manipulating price is one of the key techniques used in sales promotion by middlemen. Sales and price discounting are commonplace. Offers promising 'money off' are standard fare in virtually every store, special coupons are also used in order to promise money off a future purchase. These promotions are carefully calculated so that net cost per unit can be used to work out when the 'break even' point occurs. Total costs enable the necessary increase in volume of sales.

Other forms of discounting or cash flow manipulation are less easy to calculate. Extended credit, cash back and discounting on, for example, volume, along with late delivery penalties, retrospective cumulative volume deals and marketing funding based on the level of business are all becoming much more common. Other kinds of sales promotions can involve:

- offering more products for the same price ("50 per cent more shampoo for free!");
- cross-selling of related products (perfumes and other toiletries);
- free gifts (including coupons and 'air miles');
- products at specially discounted prices.

In the 1990s, there has been a tendency to use more 'socially responsible' kinds of promotion, for example, sales are rewarded by offering donations to a 'green' cause or aid programme.

Competitions and prizes are particularly effective examples of sales promotional tools. They are relatively inexpensive and offer the possibility of attracting high levels of interest. It may also be strategically useful to mount contests for retailers or shop assistants as part of the promotional activity put on by manufacturers to increase retail effectiveness.

Objectives of Sales Promotions

Consumer promotion and advertising act as a 'pull policy' to attract dealer attention by means of consumer demand. They are essentially short-term measures, with broadly similar objectives to above-the-line measures. The main aim is to increase sales as a consequence of generating extra interest. This may involve a number of different tactics. Promotions may aim to:

- reward loyal customers;
- 'lock' customers into loyalty programmes (e.g. collection coupons systems);
- increase pre-purchase rates of occasional users;
- illustrate new features;
- develop new uses (e.g. food products related to new recipes or combinations);
- reposition products;
- de-seasonalise sales (e.g. "turkey is not just for Christmas").

They also aim to attract new customers and encourage retailers to stock the item or, if they already do, to stock more. It is also a way to encourage slow moving lines and thereby to clear out stocks.

Strategically, sales promotions are often used in order to counter moves made by competitors and are, of course, a necessary and effective means of accompanying the launch of a new product. These techniques can also encourage the sales force to greater effort and can also supplement media advertising, although care must be taken to ensure that the effects produced by the promotion are in keeping with the strategic thrust of the above-the-line techniques.

New sales leads can be developed by gathering customer addresses – this also feeds into the development of a customer database. This is becoming a much more important means of developing the customer relationship. Relations with retailers can also be improved, promotions can be very good for simply getting customers into retail premises and can often require involvement on the part of the retailer. A promotion is essentially a limited period offer. Objectives also tend to be short-term, although they may well fit into more long-term strategies.

Targets for Sales Promotions

The main targets for sales promotional activity are *current non-users*. It is intended that the promotion will result in their undertaking a trial purchase of the product. *Existing customers* may also be targeted. Here, the aim is to increase purchase frequency or the volume of goods purchased. *Users of rival brands* are a particularly important target. Here it is intended to gain greater market share by persuading users of other brands into 'switching'.

Types of Sales Promotion

Merchandising is a very important part of sales promotion. Typically, manufacturers rely on re-seller organisations to get goods to customers. Merchandising is a method where the manufacturer tries to ensure that a retailer sells as many of his products as quickly as possible. The manufacturer therefore gives advice to the retailer, either from the sales force or from full-time merchandising specialists.

Customer-focused promotions are only one part of the sales promotional activity. Trade promotions are also very important, passing on the advantages of special terms, point-of-sale material and free pens, diaries and competition prizes, while sales force promotions can be a vital factor in motivating workers within the organisation.

Advantages

Links between sales promotions and specific marketing and communications objectives can be directly made. Diagram 4.1 illustrates the connections that can be made.

Figure 4.1: Links between promotions and specific objectives

Objective	Promotional Tools
CONSUMER PROMOTIONS	
Trial	Sampling, coupons, free draws, price off, self-liquidating, premiums, in pack, on pack, near pack, reusable containers, personality promotions.

Retrial	Coupons for next purchase, price off.
Increased Usage	Collections, games,competitions, price off multiple purchases, extra quantity/bonus packs.
New Uses	Companion brand promotions, publications.
Image	Publications, sponsorship, charity.
TRADE	
Increase Shelf Space and Display	Discount, extended credit, POS materials, tie-in with advertising.
In-store Promotional	Above, plus consumer offer plus promotion allowance.
Increase of Sales	Sales competitions and rebates (mostly independent stores/ wholesalers).
Building Good Relations	Gifts, holidays and awards.
SALES FORCE	
Sales and Distribution	Psychic income and financial income.

Source: Based on Smith, 1995

Communication Aims of Sales Promotions

Sales promotions need to achieve a number of specific communication aims if they are to succeed. To work, they must be:

- seen and known about;
- perceived as interesting and desirable;
- understood;
- believed;
- seen to be relevant;
- persuasive;
- capable of producing the desired response.

The Use of Personal Selling

Salespeople are a vital part of the activities of any organisation, but in some they lie at the very heart of the marketing communication process. Sales as a department is stigmatised and salespeople are often distrusted, but in industrial markets, or any high-value, specialised areas where customers are involved in making a large investment and require specialist services, salespeople are essential. Often, however, they are very much neglected and marginalised in relation to the other parts of the marketing communication process and, consequently, are not used to maximum effect. Personal selling may be appropriate when there is:

- a situation of high, perceived risk;
- commercially complex negotiations;
- an industrial/organisational market.

Setting up a sales department involves a number of different stages.

1. **Developing a personal selling plan** is the first element.
    This involves considering the way the commercial objectives of the company can be pursued by using personal selling and how this relates to the other marketing communication techniques that the company needs to employ.

2. **Setting objectives** is the first stage.
    These are obviously derived from the strategic plan developed at corporate level. This will have been used to produce a marketing plan.

3. **Assigning responsibility** for the various functions involved in the department is also crucial.
    Deciding on area coverage, establishing levels of authority, drawing up the responsibilities of all members at every level.

4. **Establishing a budget** is clearly essential.
    Personal selling is effective and entirely appropriate for some markets, but it is resource intensive – heavy on the time, investment of effort and, consequently, the cost invested in each sale. In industrial marketing, for example, a salesman may invest between ten and twenty hours on calls before a sale is finalised. Although the profits per sale make this sensible, it

actually represents a very high cost indeed and this needs to be carefully calculated and monitored.

5. **Determining the types of sales positions** is important because all sales staff do not serve the same functions.
    The types of sales staff needed must be worked out carefully, after reviewing the different needs within the organisation.

6. **Selecting a sales technique** is often something worked out at corporate level.
    Training and standardisation of the sales technique is now commonplace in companies dependent on the quality of their sales staff to maintain competitiveness.

7. **Outlining sales tasks** is essential in the starting up process, so that sales staff know what is expected of them.
    Often this is much more than simply selling the product. They are also working as part of a team and this has implications for what they do and how they do it.

8. **Applying the plan** is the last stage of this process.
    To make it work, it may be necessary to work together and refine the previously developed selling plan, monitoring and feeding back information to facilitate long-term development.

Functions Fulfilled by Salespeople

The sales department is not simply concerned with selling. Sales people provide the 'interface' with customers and, as a consequence, have to deal with a whole range of different problems the customer may raise, before and after sales. Also of course, they are gathering large amounts of information about their customers. This involves building up a relationship with the customer over time. Typical activities associated with sales personnel include:

*   **servicing**: actual closing of sales accounts for about 5 per cent of an operator's time. Taking care of the customer, and servicing their needs, is a much larger proportion since this is such an important part of building up the relationship;
*   **prospecting**: gathering new leads or developing information about customer needs is also a key part of sales person's job;

- **information gathering**: building up the kind of profile and understanding of the customer. It is important to remember that, for example, industrial buying usually involves groups, rather than just a single individual and each member may have a critical input and this is clearly important for selling success. Most organisations seek to have such information fed into the system so that other members of the organisation can benefit (not least of whom are the successors to sales staff who leave!);
- **communicating**: this is what sales is most crucially about. The sales person represents the company for the customer and indeed many other people in a number of different ways. The representative 'acts for' the company but the representative also stands for the company and how they behave conveys an image or personality for the company for those with whom they come into contact. As Tom Peters has pointed out, interactions with every customer actually form part of a long-term relationship and this relationship can potentially involve a large number of sales over a long period of time. Bad communications, or failure to relate to the customer's needs, means that not just one sale will be lost but a string of sales, involving potentially very large sums of money. Also it is clear that the effectiveness of company marketing and communication strategy hangs upon the way messages are communicated by the salespeople. For this reason, communication skills of a very high order are essential to the success of a sales programme.
- **allocating**: this may not appear to be a significant area, but again, it is part of the way in which the relation with the customer base is managed. In some situations, it will clearly not be possible, given limited resources and ever more pressure on margins in a highly competitive market, to deliver products and services to all clients without making decisions about the most effective way of deploying products, resources and effort given inevitable constraints. Problems (such as who should be given products that are in short supply or whose contract needs to be fulfilled in order to maintain good relations, etc.) can only be decided with the specialist and detailed knowledge of markets and customers a good salesperson swiftly develops.

How Salespeople Operate

It is sometimes said that good salesmanship is a personal quality and cannot really be taught. While it seems to be true that good salespeople often possess particular inter-personal skills, it is also true that good training and an effective system are extremely important factors in successful sales performance. Achieving a successful out-come is not something utterly unique on every occasion. There are certainly aspects of every sale that can be iden-tified and described as 'good practice'. Good sales staff tend to follow a regular pattern. Sales staff also improve their technique with experience and can pass on techniques which work and advice about those which do not. The sales sequence involves the following stages.

1. **Preparation**
   The effective salesperson needs certain kinds of information in order to perform effectively.

   - Company knowledge is essential if the salesperson is to be able to formulate and deliver appropriate information. For example, delivery of any selling proposition that the sales person presents to the prospective customer must be within the capabilities of the company.
   - Product knowledge is also crucial. One of the great virtues of personal selling is the complexity of the information that can be presented to the prospective client, the capacity to respond to requests for information and to act immediately on the basis of feedback.
   - Market knowledge, including awareness of com-petitor activity and appreciation of the context where the customer is making the decision is obviously vital to the formulation and deliverance of marketing communications by sales staff.

   Sales staff acquire customer knowledge over time but, even before coming into contact with customers, the good salesman is prepared by learning as much as possible about the firm and the individuals involved in it. This forms an important basis for positive relationships. In addition, it helps promote feelings of trust and confidence more quickly and may open up areas that otherwise would take time to develop. It is also important to remember that sales staff may have to deal with a number of different people within the firm. Industrial buying often involves buying teams and it is important for sales staff to understand how these groups are constituted and what the dynamics are within the workplace.

- Equipment, samples and sales aids are more and more important these days, as sales staff must have very strong presentation skills. Much presentation work these days involves developing a competence with new information technology and being able to prepared and use, for example, multimedia presentation programmes and hardware, including sound and video as well as computer programmes.

2. **The approach**

How the approach is made depends very much on the setting, the nature of the business and the industry it operates within, the part of the world the business is taking on and the personality and tactics favoured by the individual salesperson. This is partly, of course, a matter of the personal 'method' of the sales staff but it is also about looking for 'cues' and responses from the client-to-be. Many training programmes undergone by sales staff will include effective approach methods.

3. **The presentation (and/or) demonstration**

Again, most company training programmes for sales staff will include carefully worked out presentation sequences, based on marketing communication messages (the selling proposition or appeal) decided on by those responsible for marketing strategy. In many cases, these involve materials and equipment requiring special skills for effective usage. Information technology, for example, has made great advances in the development of multimedia presentational software.

4. **Negotiation**

After the presentation/demonstration, sales staff will enter into a stage of negotiation with the potential customer. This will involve developing an acceptable package of terms (such as price, payment sequence, guarantees and service support, programmes of re-negotiation and updating, etc.). Often, the 'room for manoeuvre' concept is applied. Sales staff will be given the facility to work within certain parameters. An initial set of conditions can, in fact, be modified in accordance with the underlying factors (e.g. re-scheduling repay-ments or modifying the terms or conditions of repayment in other ways).

5.   **Closing**

Closing techniques are extremely important for the sales person. These refer to the ability to complete a sale, to succeed in getting the customer committed to the business transaction involved by signing a contract, making a payment, etc. In order to provide sales staff with the ability to overcome resistance, deal with obstacles and counteract the objections and contingencies which will affect clients, sales people are trained in the use of techniques that will minimise their effect or turn them to advantage. This means building in a number of different ways of closing a sale, which can be called up according to how the situation is read. These include, in a typical close sequence, the following alternatives.

- Basic close.
- Alternative choice.
- 'Puppy dog' technique.
- Summary question.
- Similar situation.
- Sharp angle.
- Final objective.

After-sales service is particularly important in certain sorts of personal selling. Industrial markets, for example, often involve very high cost products and services, which are purchased in order that the company can operate and, as a consequence, high risks are involved. Most contracts in these circumstances would require a commitment from the seller/supplier to make sure that the goods and services purchased will be reliably provided whatever the eventuality. Guarantees of continuity are a very important element here.

Specific Personal Selling Objectives

Given the variety of market situations, and also the various ways selling may fit into a marketing plan, a number of different types of sales objective may be pursued.

- **Demand-oriented** sales objectives are concerned with conveying information in order to explain fully all product and service attributes, to answer any questions raised and to probe for further questions that the customers may have.

- **Persuasion** as a sales objective seeks to distinguish clearly the product/service from competitors, to maximise the number of sales as percentage of presentations, to convert undecided customers into buyers, to sell complementary items (e.g. film with camera, sunroof with car, etc.) or to placate dissatisfied customers.
- **Reminding** is important as a sales objective in order to ensure delivery, installation, etc., to follow up the product to be used to follow up when re-purchase is near or to reassure previous customers when making a new purchase.
- **Image-oriented** sales objectives address the needs of industry and company to maintain a good appearance by all personnel in contact with the customers and to follow acceptable sales practice.

The responsibilities of a sales manager play a vital part in the achievement of communications objectives within the company. The manager forms an interface between the corporate and marketing objectives of the company as a whole and the development of tactics and personnel capable of delivering them within the company. The main responsibilities of the sales manager are to:

- understand the company's objectives, strategies, market position and basic marketing plan and to convey them to the sales force;
- identify a sales philosophy/policy, sales force characteristics, selling tasks, a sales organisation and a method of customer contact;
- develop and update sales forecasts;
- allocate selling resources based on sales forecasts and company needs;
- recruit, train, assign, compensate and supervise sales personnel;
- synchronise sales functions with advertising, product planning, distribution, market research and production;
- assess sales performance by the sales staff, product line, customer, customer group and geographic area;
- monitor continuously competitor actions.

Finding the right kind of candidates is a critical problem for a sales manager. As mentioned earlier, there is a prevailing belief that good salespeople are 'born, not made' and finding the right kind of people is therefore the main task of the manager. Research has suggested that, while there are no clear-cut indicators to distinguish sales people from others, there are certain kinds of desirable traits. Personnel experts believe that the main factors involved in successful selling are:

- high motivation to persuade others;
- empathy with clients;
- resilience after losing a potential sale.

In addition, personal selling involves high costs. Salespeople working in industrial markets are highly paid and, although individual sales also generate high returns, the preliminary work in the form of visits made to sales prospects is extremely costly and also speculative, since a fairly high percentage of calls do not actually translate into sales.

Types of Sales Personnel

Not all salespeople are of the same kind. Clearly, salespeople in some situations have to break new ground and find custom where none exists while, in others, it is a matter of keeping customers who are already committed and keeping them serviced.

- **Order takers**: process routine orders, provide clerical functions, handle pre-sold items and maintain sales. They also take information on items taken from stock, enabling the firm to restock items, they can answer simple questions and complete transactions. As a consequence they require little training and compensation and tend to have little or limited expertise or enthusiasm;

- **Order getters**: on the other hand, have a more demanding and dynamic role in the marketing communications process. They generate orders and re-orders, build up customer leads and persuade customers to buy the product or service. They are required to handle high-priced/complex items and to increase sales. This type of sales work is creative. They arrange displays and presentations. They are generally less involved with routine tasks, but as individuals they require a lot of training and compensation in the form or payment, bonuses and conditions of work. Good salespeople are highly expert and enthusiastic.

There are many reasons for using personal selling. It is flexible, involves relatively little waste, in terms of effort exerted on each customer, compared to mass methods of marketing/selling/communication. Unlike many other types of marketing, selling closes sales and provides fast feedback on communication with customers. However, it does have some significant limitations and drawbacks. It reaches a relatively *limited audience*, and has *high per customer costs*. In addition it generally *creates little awareness* outside the limited audience and generally has *a poor image*.

REASONS TO BE FEARFUL – MAKE THAT SALE!!!

Here's how to make those sales, make your supervisor proud of you and make everyone else in the office green with envy. It's a simple trick, but only one salesperson in a thousand seems to use it, either because they don't know about it or can't seem to find the time to practise it.

Look back on the day you've just had. Pick out one particular call – any one you like so long as it didn't lead to a sale! Pick out one where a sale was possible but you just didn't make it. OK?

Now, take out a notebook. This works best when you have just been on the call and the details (gory or otherwise) are fresh in your mind. Write down what you remember of the non-sale and then, when you are alone, look through the notes. If you want to see progress, it's probably best to pick one where you feel you were close to closing but didn't quite do it.

This is where the scalpel comes out and the autopsy can start. Dissecting every aspect of the call, break it down in terms of the following guide. Write the numbers down, visualise what happened at each stage of the presentation and pick out the parts where you feel you really didn't perform as you should have. Here is the Golden List.

THE GOLDEN RULES
FOR NOT CLOSING A SALE

- Too many interruptions. I couldn't make my pitch. I should have made another appointment.
- Talking about features and not benefits.
- What we need.
- I didn't carry him with me by checking off a 'yes' after each benefit.
- I came across as a technical 'nerd'. He looked bored and wasn't interested.
- My presentation didn't catch fire, was static and unenthusiastic.
- I paid no attention to his objections and worries and so didn't treat them as problems. I snapped at him for annoying and interrupting my spiel.
- I failed to qualify the objection by obtaining his agreement that it was the only one and so allowed him to move on to other problems.
- He got annoyed when I disagreed with him directly instead of saying, "Some people say that..."
- I didn't sort out the real from the phoney objections.
- I didn't take his partner into account – she really makes the decisions.
- I just didn't know enough about the product so that I could punch it across as something he couldn't do without!
- I never asked for the business; I didn't force the issue and apply a powerful 'close' but hoped that the product would 'speak for itself'.
- I gave up when he said "no" the first time.
- I didn't work out what the key benefit was to this person specifically.
- I talked far too much and didn't listen to gauge reactions and mood and mindset.
- I didn't really believe I was going to make the sale from the beginning.
- [Other reason that you can think of for not making the sale.]

If the sale didn't happen, there must be at least one cross next to one of the above reasons. That doesn't mean much in itself but when you do it for a week or two, and you see a pattern emerging, you know where to start on the road to recovery.

If you can use it properly, with as much detachment and objectivity as you can muster, this list will turn your failures into commissions. Any sales executive with the right training knows how to remedy these kinds of faults when they occur just like any kind of bad habit, however, they creep up on the unsuspecting and we must be vigilant!

4.1.   *Explain the difference between 'features' and 'benefits' using a product you are familiar with from your own experience. Break down the benefits you feel would be important to selling this product to a particular customer. Define the customer.*

4.2.   *Outline alternative ways in sales areas may be divided up. Describe the reasons behind this decision and the advantages and disadvantages associated with each method.*

4.3.   *What, in your opinion, are the main attributes required of a good salesperson? Which of the suggestions outlined in the 'golden rules' are essential to a good salesperson? What aspects of a good salesperson are not included on this list?*

4.4   *Describe the main problems faced by salespeople and, critically, evaluate the effectiveness of the system used. Illustrate this by reference to a company you know.*

4.5   *What are your own reactions to the techniques employed by salespeople? Which of these do you think are the most effective?*

5

PUBLICITY AND PUBLIC RELATIONS

What is 'PR'? What is 'Publicity'?

According to the American showman Silas Barnum, "All publicity is good publicity." Despite its beguiling simplicity, this aphorism seems very dubious indeed in these complex times.

Furthermore, there is a widespread tendency to assume that anything that appears in the news, whether on television or in the press, which brings to public attention a company, product or individual, is all part of 'publicity', 'public relations' and promotion in general. Few people can distinguish the differences between these types of event or have ever had those differences explained to them; but different they are.

Public Relations

> *The deliberate, planned and sustained effort to establish and maintain mutual understanding between an organisation and its public. (Institute of Public Relations)*

Public relations is concerned with managing perceptions of the behaviour of the organisation, its products, services and individuals giving rise to publicity. Unlike publicity, which arises as a result of information being broadcast or disseminated in an uncontrolled way, this is a result of information being made known deliberately. PR aims at controllable effects on specific publics.

Public relations arises from the need for communications with 'publics' to be planned in terms of specific objectives, enabling a degree of control to be enforced, since it builds in targets and forces the planner to think systematically about the ways these are to be achieved. Public relations is not simply a 'sub' domain of marketing, but exists separately and is often carried on independently of marketing as such.

Publics for Public Relations

Publics include the following groups, among others.

1. The community.
2. Employees.
3. Government.
4. The financial community.
5. Distributors.
6. Consumers.
7. Opinion leaders.
8. Media.

Publicity

Publicity is defined as being any form of non-paid, non-personal communication and, like advertising, it involves dealing with a mass audience. Although some components are 'paid for', we can also include public relations under this general heading, since it is concerned more generally with building and maintaining an understanding between the organisation and the general public.

Benefits of publicity are various. Good publicity can improve and complement key features of marketing communication with no major time costs. Publicity generally affords access to large audiences. Because the perceived origin of the message is not directly associated with the company concerned, it has high message credibility.

Distinguishing Marketing, 'PR', Publicity and Press Releases

Public relations is the development of good relation with a variety of groups inside and outside of the organisation who are sometimes referred to as 'publics' (see above).

Marketing traditionally focuses on just three of these publics related to the market.

• Customers.
• Distributors and the rest of the industry.
• Competitors.

It is, however, difficult to control since the media concerned are generally involved in transmitting messages for purposes of news coverage or matters of general interest and are not sponsored to transmit marketing communications messages.

Messages will get to the media involved by means of press releases. These may well be used in their original form, but are often used in a truncated or edited format, with counter messages added or the original message passed on in an ineffective way.

Sponsorship is another means of getting publicity. This has become extremely important as a way of improving corporate image by association of unlikely or unglamorous enterprises with sport or entertainment events. One of the most important by-products of sponsorship is that brand or corporate names will be seen on television as part of displays within sports or music venues, by live audiences and those watching on television.

When simply introducing the name to new audiences is a major corporate objective (for instance within the early stages of the product life cycle or when the intended target market is being changed or extended), sponsorship is a highly effective method. New moves, such as sponsorship of teams and star athletes, and placing the name of the sponsor actually on the clothing worn by the athletes ensures that the name is seen by a very large number of people whenever the athlete takes part in a competition.

PR is also important in trying to control distributor and customer relations. These are key publics, both for the marketer and also for the corporate strategist on a broader scale. 'Pre-selling' can influence the attitudes of potential customers, as well as confidence and image building taking place in the realm of publicity and public relations.

Figure 5.1: PR Techniques for Effective Communication with Stakeholders and Customers

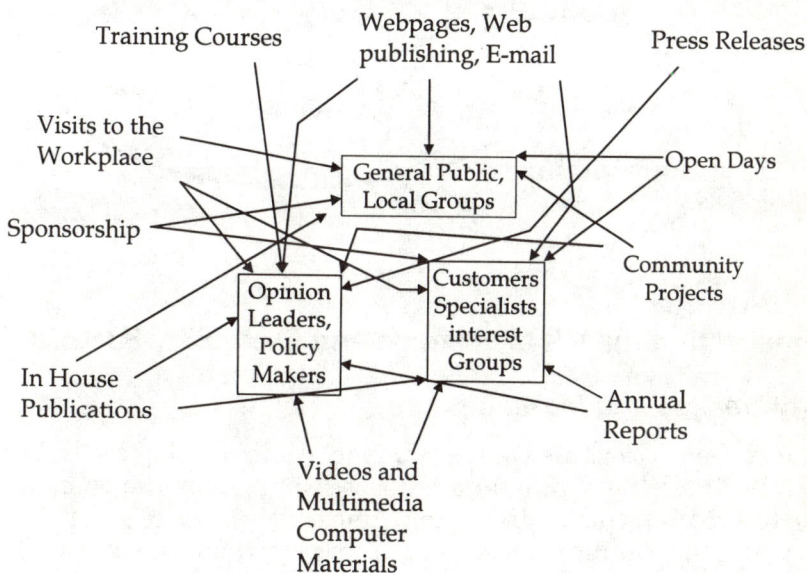

Often, corporate citizenship and the public image of the company are more important than anything else and it is here that public relations comes into its own. It stretches far beyond simply marketing and is involved in the execution of corporate strategies of many different kinds. Techniques of public relations are obviously going to be important in relation to long-term objectives of the company (for example, in its relations to government, legislators and those involved in creating the climate and conditions where the company operates).

The PR Mix

As with other aspects of the marketing communications process, this involves integrating the various techniques being applied. Figure 5.2 indicates the ways various kinds of public relations techniques can be integrated.

Figure 5.2: PR Diagram

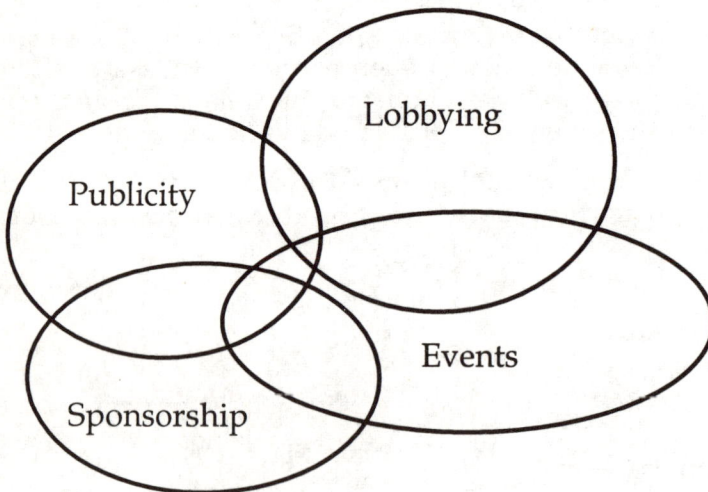

Integrating the PR Mix: Image and Credibility Factors

Awareness and Messages

Most theorists agree that it is important to develop credibility and establish a strong and respected image for the company before attempting to disseminate messages or raise awareness in various publics concerning the profile of the company.

Above all, it is important to think about the way the various aspects of the tactics employed relate to each other. For example, if athletes are sponsored, does the image of the team the individual or the nature of the sport, fit in with the aims being pursued in other parts of the corporate programme of public relations?

The Effects of the Media

Publicity, in the form of press releases, is a very important source of material and information for the media themselves, so that the relationship between business and the communications industry is by no means one-sided. Most press releases are so ill-conceived, however, that they cannot be used. Apart from press releases, the main methods used to appeal to the media are news releases appropriate for the various media (video for television, audio for radio), press conferences, press receptions, and events aiming to attract media attention ('publicity stunts'). Conferences and seminars (see above) fulfill the same kinds of functions.

One of the main aims of this kind of activity is to build up good press and media relations. This requires a good grasp of the nature of media interests and also the ability to provide stories, items and 'copy' which can satisfy journalistic criteria. Note the problem of control over the end product, however, and the danger that it may not be helpful and may even be counter-productive.

In order to achieve coverage of the right kind in the media it is necessary to:

- identify the correct 'target' media;
- formulate press releases to satisfy media criteria for use;
- make sure the releases get to the right person at the right time;
- respond to press queries quickly and effectively.

If this is done well it can be highly profitable. The column inches achieved by well executed publicity and public relations would be, in the vast majority of cases, far more expensive to buy than the cost incurred in deploying PR manpower and carrying out the tasks involved in satisfying the demands of the media.

At the same time, this can be far more powerful, in some ways, than other types of marketing communication, since it is perceived to be objective and the product of a journalist. As a consequence, messages may be considered more believable. The lack of control makes this more risky, however.

Controlling the PR Mix

Lack of control can be countered by careful co-ordination of various aspects of the mix and identification of any events or stories might compromise the integrity of the story being floated in the press releases, and so on. Checking on the background and past record of journalists contacted can also be a powerful aid, and this is possible through the recent introduction of databases providing information about those involved in receiving and acting on publicity material.

As we said earlier, close integration with other aspects of the communications mix is essential. Each activity can be used as a counterpoint, but also as a part of the practice of others (for example, using press cuttings as part of advertising, using material from events and conferences as part of display material at exhibitions, and so on). Perfect campaigns look to integration at the earliest stages of planning for the separate elements and good practice means thinking about how activity here will bear upon what is done elsewhere.

At the end of the day, it is important that the effect and consequences of what has been done should be capable of measurement and this is more easily done here than in many areas of communication. In the case of newspaper coverage, column inches can be physically measured, as can the number and duration of news items on radio and television. It is also possible to categorise the kinds of coverage given by the media and respond accordingly.

As a matter of course, many modern companies use media monitoring services to record, measure and evaluate the kinds of effects campaigns of PR have upon the corporate life of the company. This, of course, focuses on the press and how they have responded to PR activity. The final outcome, the effect on customers and other target publics, needs to be measured by means of a survey of some kind, seeking to examine changes in attitudes and behaviour among the relevant groups.

"GRIMEWALD – THE NEW PONG ON THE BLOCK!"

The name may sound old but this is one variety that didn't feature in the famous cheese shop sketch by the Monty Python team – because it's brand new. The world of cheese making is a staid old place at the best of times, but the arrival of a new variety has stirred the interest of everyone. And it's British to boot!

Grimewald is a full fat, soft cheese with a strong flavour (very like the French Gruyere) and a distinctive mottled blue appearance. It is made in the Grime Valley in Cheshire, home of cheese makers since the Middle Ages, but this is the first new variety of cheese produced in Britain for nearly 200 years!

This is an exciting event for cheese makers then but, thanks to a piece of brilliant marketing, it has caught the public imagination too. PR expert Gareth Cheeseman sounded confident as he discussed the massive media coverage his campaigning has brought about.

> *We realised that in order to compete with established shelf fillers like Edam and Cheddar we would have to reach not just the cheese-eating public but the retailers who don't want their shelves filled with products that no one has heard of. They have to be persuaded to try. So we concentrated on publicity and public relations in the pre-launch period.*

The campaign was so successful that it attracted features on local and national news programmes amounting to hundreds of minutes in airtime, mostly concentrating on the novelty of the new product and the historic nature of the innovation.

The company has also sponsored a balloon in the trans-Siberian 'Winds Of Change' race, forming part of the team put together by playboy entrepreneur Richard Brandy. Again, this has attracted great attention, since the team itself is concerned to put across the message of "tradition and innovation – British is Best". Brandy has enjoyed a high profile throughout his career and has been a minority shareholder in the Grimewald project from the beginning.

MD Roger Bullock was very positive about the results so far.

> *We are a small company and we have to make our marketing communications spend count. At this stage, the use of press to reach both retailers and our target customer group has been very successfiul, with widespread press and television coverage for minimum outlay. We shall try to build on the very successful launch period exposure gained for this product.*

Who knows what lies in store for this product in the future in a very tough market. But at the moment, the order books are full and everyone is smiling. Say "CHEESE"!!

5.1   *What were the management of Grimewald trying to achieve with their use of publicity and public relations? Did they succeed?*

5.2   *What do you think were the main messages being communicated in this campaign?*

5.3   *What are the main drawbacks, for the company, from this sort of campaign?*

5.4   *Distinguish between 'public relations' and 'publicity' as used here. Describe the uses and some possible alternatives.*

5.5   *You are attempting to launch a new brand of environmentally friendly shaving cream onto the shelves of supermarkets. Brainstorm some possible publicity campaigns you might consider running, with an outline of your objectives and the methods you would use to achieve them.*

6
DIRECT MARKETING; SPONSORSHIP; EXHIBITIONS

Defining Direct Marketing

> *An interactive system of marketing which uses one or more advertising media to effect a measurable response at any location. (US Direct Marketing Association)*

Sometimes referred to as 'armchair shopping' this area of marketing, after entering the doldrums following the heyday of shopping catalogues in the 1950s and 1960s in the UK, has very much come back in to its own with the advent of IT and the proliferation of credit sources. Direct marketing is now becoming a new kind of activity. Customers are now seen not as prospects for a single purchase, but potential buyers for a string of goods and services.

The aim, for modern direct marketers is to form a 'relationship' with the consumers, whose needs and wants are inferred from electronic profiles derived from database information. Marketers use various IT-based technologies to communicate information about products and services to meet those needs to precisely identified individuals and households. Because of the centrality of database information in this process, it is sometimes referred to as database marketing, precision marketing, niche marketing or relationship marketing.

The following elements are often confused with direct marketing itself but are only part of the overall system.

- Direct mail.
- Telemarketing.
- Door to door selling:
  - pyramid;
  - multi-level;
  - network retailing;
  - field sales force operatives.
- Advertising for direct response.
- Shopping via the internet.
- Home shopping networks.

- Miscellaneous others including 'stuffers', 'inserters' and house to house leaflet drops.

Direct Marketing and Database Marketing

It is important to emphasise the distinctiveness of database marketing (DBM). It communicates directly with customers, uses a variety of media and requires customer responses allowing the company to take some kind of action.

The essential character of database marketing is interaction. It can be defined as an interactive system of marketing using one or more of the marketing communication media to identify the needs and location of target groups, to formulate an appropriate appeal or appeals and to effect a measurable response and/or transaction to those appeals.

DBM is not simply a more sophisticated way of using the post, however. It extends beyond communications into marketing planning and strategy formulation, since it is based on new possibilities in the storage, retrieval, access and manipulation of information, using computer-based technologies. This is not simply the triumph of the silicon chip; it is also a process in which the means to use those technologies has become ever more widespread because of their diminishing cost, user-friendliness and ubiquity.

History and Development of DBM

As we have already said, DBM is derived from two trends: *technological developments* (especially the development of micro-technologies) and *socio-economic changes* (in the use of time within households (i.e. 'time famines'), priorities in the organisation of households (i.e. social roles of men, women and children), and the lifestyles enjoyed by most people (i.e. the consumer society).

Basic DBM Requirements

In order that direct marketing can function to provide its citizens with whatever they need, a number of requirements must be satisfied. To operate, a direct marketing system in modern markets must have the following components available to it.

- A relational database, which can draw information from different files linked by a common field.

Figure 6.1: The Nature of a Database (based on Shaw & Stone: *Database Marketing* [1988])

1. Each actual or potential customer is identified as an individual record on the marketing database.
2. Each customer record contains not only identification and access information (e.g. name and address) but also a range of marketing information.
3. The information is available to the company during the process of each transaction with the customer, to enable it to decide how to respond to the customer's needs.
4. The database is used to record responses of customers to company initiatives.
5. The information is also available to marketing policy makers to enable them to make decisions about the product and marketing mix most suitable for each target market identified.
6. In large corporations, selling many products to each customer, the database is used to ensure that the approach to the customer is co-ordinated and that a consistent approach is developed.
7. The information on the database, which has been built up over time, will gradually reduce the need for market research. Marketing campaigns are derived such that the response of customers to the campaign provides the information the company is seeking.
8. Marketing management automation is developed to handle the vast amount of information generated by DBM. Although no company has yet achieved this level of sophistication, many are adopting it as their goal.

- A query language by which to access the database.
- A high quality output device, e.g. a laser printer.
- Software for:
  - market segmentation analysis;
  - forecasting;
  - merging geo-demographic and psychographic data.

Various technologies facilitating the development of DBM have also been built up. The main factors are, first of all, *hardware developments.* The speed and cheapness of the computer hardware available has profoundly affected the development of the trade. *Communications developments,* data communications at low costs, better data integration and access allied with software developments have all played a key part. These include:

- database management systems;
- custom systems;
- sundry technologies;
- printing technologies (mailshots);
- telephone communications.

Marketing developments cannot be ignored. The main factors leading to the growth of direct marketing, the growing use of databases in order to identify the customer and formulate a communications strategy for satisfying their needs are:

- the fragmentation/de-massification of markets;
- a general decline of brand loyalty;
- the proliferation of products;
- the rise of the service economy;
- a new need for 'relationship' marketing.

Effects on Corporate Strategy

The rise of these new forms of marketing has profoundly affected the ways in which corporate strategists think. In the past, marketing strategies have been dominated by the idea of the *unique selling proposition* ('building a better mousetrap'). Now corporate marketing is accepting what was the small business philosophy of staying close to customers, understanding and meeting their needs and treating them well after the sale. This is undoubtedly because of changes in the markets themselves. Customers are much more discerning than in the past, when mass markets were built on the idea of constant novelty and change. At the same time, many markets are saturated; competition has increased to such a degree that consumers are able to pick and choose between alternatives in the same area. The result is that success depends on identifying the needs for a product to satisfy, which differentiates it clearly from its competitors, and effectively communicating that difference. The dominance of the unique selling proposition has been overtaken by the idea of service and the relationship with the consumer. These can only be effectively managed, in globalised, geographically dispersed markets, by using information technologies in the communication process.

Precision marketing is another term for this approach. It involves long-term loyalty building, based on knowledge of the customer and the lifestyle that customer pursues, and the ability to react quickly when the situation in the dynamic marketplace, changes.

In order to make the customer aware that you exist and that you are worth dealing with, this form of marketing places mass communication, in a variety of guises including press and television work, at the very top of the agenda. Increased television, press and radio advertising costs are consequently involved.

The declining effectiveness of these media. The cost effectiveness of using such media, particularly in small or business to business settings, is highly dubious for some enterprises. The main issue of course, is wastage.

Using mass media involves a high degree of built in redundancy. On the one hand, the 'reach' of these media is so great that a very large number of people are exposed to a message having, in many cases, relevance to only a small proportion. At the same time, the contents of such messages tend, more and more, to be filtered out by the overwhelming majority of recipients, on the grounds of irrelevance and 'information overload'.

Tactical applications of the approach. Given increasingly crowded and competitive markets, consumers are faced with greater and greater ranges of choice. Reasons for choosing one product rather than another then, may revolve around factors relatively remote from the characteristics of the product per se. Service elements, previously thought of as more remote, have been foregrounded.

Customer loyalty and care programmes have become much more common and are now seen as part of an ongoing focus on the development of the relationship with the customer. Information gathered in the course of direct marketing can be used to identify and develop responses to customer needs. These also, of course, serve as an important resource for *generating and qualifying sales leads.* In the *cross-selling of other company products* this kind of information can also, of course, open up other avenues for serving customer needs.

Direct marketing is also an effective way in order to build up *price/promotion testing.* Modifications in various aspects of the marketing mix can be introduced to specific groups and the effects on sales monitored very accurately.

The use of direct marketing as part of the development of *marketing strategy* is clearly very important indeed. It provides a way of building long-term relationships with customers. It also reduces the need for market research, since it allows campaigns to be designed to obtain required information. It can, effectively, *drive* marketing policy.

Using IT to Gain Competitive Advantage

According to Michael Porter's (1985) framework, information technology (IT) as part of the practice of direct marketing can play an extremely powerful role in the development of corporate strategy and tactics. Information may be used to:

* change the basis of competition;
* strengthen the customer relationship;
* strengthen the position with the supplier;
* build barriers to new entrants;
* generate new or substitute products.

A more recent development in this area is *data warehousing.*

This is a collection of information from many different sources, such as EPOS, billing, sales and customer service. This body of data is organised specifically to make it easy to perform online queries. Information is stored in a way analogous to products stacked in a warehouse, so that an 'order' can be retrieved for a customer according to their need. Supermarkets for example, can analyse cash register data to discover what customers typically buy at the same time. This information can then be used to devise better floor and shelf layouts.

Wal-Mart, a US pioneer in data warehousing, used sales figures to discover that beer and nappy sales both rose on Friday evenings. This is as a consequence of young fathers going out to shop for a weekend taking care of the kids. They used this information to reorganise their stores so that beer and nappies are located close together in Wal-Mart stores.

Valued Customers

Organisations can discriminate between valued customers, whom they want to retain, and those who are less likely to be valuable over the long-term using the information available to them through database records kept as part of direct marketing. Airlines, for example, use database records to upgrade frequent customers to first class in preference to occasional travellers.

This information is also useful for planning. British Airways, for example, uses a data warehouse to help it make decisions in issues such as what mix of fares should be used on particular routes.

Direct mail effectiveness is also keenly dependent on the quality of the information available to it. Data warehouses can improve direct mail response rates by permitting more discrimination about targets.

Typical Techniques of Using Data

Input data from, for example, electronic point-of-sale data machines (EPOS) – bar codes read by cash registers – can be simplified. Even with very fast analysis, it is important to simplify data by classifying it into segments that describe the behaviour of particular groups or customers. According to one analyst:

> At the outset of working with Tesco there was criticism that there would be too much detail. But once you build segment strategies, it becomes manageable.
> (Clive Humby, strategy director of Dunn-Humby Associates.)

The sheer volume of information being gathered necessitates 'slicing the data' in particular ways. 'Data mining' techniques include:

* neural networks;
* genetic algorithms;
* rule induction;
* decision trees;
* data visualisation.

Segmentation based on database information can also be accomplished in more imaginative and effective ways. Markets may be segmented, for example, according to:

* potential to spend;
* whether they use the store for principal or top-up purchases;
* whether they are more sensitive to price or promotions.

Studies of database usage show that direct mail is the single biggest use for data. After a study of 500 UK companies, the Henley Management Centre reported that "database marketing is one of the hottest topics in the marketing community".

In a 1995 study by the Manchester School of Management, all respondents in 100 companies planned to use IT-driven (direct) marketing within the next five years. Over half expect it to become their main promotional method.

Some companies have had bad experiences with technology in the past, however. Some are put off by the speed with technology is moving. Twenty-five per cent of respondents in the Manchester study thought that "...an increased reliance on IT for analysis has been at the expense of intuition and judgement".

Cultivating the Customer: Exhibitions

Exhibitions represent the other end of the spectrum of marketing communications. They involve direct, face to face contact with customers in a very old fashioned way. An exhibition is a public event organised by an independent organisation. Businesses attend them and present their products and/or services to those attending. Consumer goods exhibitions, such as the 'Ideal Home' exhibition in the UK, may be designed to appeal to a very broad audience or for precisely identified and targeted audiences, such as those concerned with highly specialised machinery, or some specific aspect of marketing, such as packaging or advertising.

Conferences are very similar to exhibitions and may be conducted in parallel. They differ, however, in the kinds of facilities available. Exhibitions have fine facilities for displaying goods and services, whereas conferences are generally aimed at sharing knowledge through speeches without the addition of product displays. Exhibitions are much more clearly focused on selling than conferences.

Seminars, having some things in common with both, tend to be run as private, exclusive occasions. Many are held on the premises of particular companies. They are usually small scale (compared to the other two) and focus on solving problems and disseminating and exchanging information related to products.

Selling Factors

All three of these events involve selling in different ways. Con-ferences are concerned with the 'soft sell'. The prestige of the company is enhanced by establishing representatives as 'expert voices', but this has an indirect impact on selling.

Exhibitions provide an excellent opportunity for establishing contacts and, for example, passing on communications about products or portfolios within a company, but still fall short of actually selling. Seminars are much more directly in the control of one organisation and are often a very effective forum where selling can take place.

Effective Use of Exhibitions

Typically, exhibitions will only be mounted where they repre-sent a realistic occasion to mobilise the relevant audience or, for example, prospective investors. This will, then, represent the possibility of a healthy return on the costs of staging the exhibition.

Individual exhibitors – the companies who take part – have little control, as individuals, over whether or not the exhibition will actually take place. It is important to recognise that the opportunity to use exhibitions, then, depends on other people putting them on.

Selecting an exhibition depends, first, on identifying those likely to attract audiences with whom you would wish to communicate. This means going very carefully through the prospectuses of what the very large numbers of conferences available typically offer. There are huge numbers of such exhibitions in highly specialised areas. Those aimed to appeal to the general public are, in fact, less common than the more specialised events.

Examples of consumer type exhibitions would include:

* computing and software exhibitions;
* travel exhibitions;
* interior decoration;
* arts and handicrafts;
* sports exhibitions;
* hobbies and games.

Reasons for Participation

Obviously, a well-chosen exhibition will give a company access to the group it wishes to target. In addition, these key individuals will be in the correct receptive frame of mind to take on board the messages being communicated. They have invested time and effort and spent money in order to attend the exhibitions. This should be taken as an indication of a high level of motivation and they are highly attractive prospects and contacts for the company in question. Contact-making is a key objective for the companies concerned.

Exhibitions are also a magnet for media; press and broadcasting media representatives will attend and messages being given out about new products, for example, will get good media coverage. Exhibitions are often chosen as occasions on whoch to launch new products, because of the high profile platform they provide – for example, motor shows are often used as occasions to present new models to the trade, the press and the wider public, They are also used in order to provide a 'showcase' for future developments and to present 'concepts' which indicate what future models will look like and the features they will include.

When companies are launching themselves into a new market or into a new region of the world, exhibitions provide an excellent way for a company to make itself and its products known.

Companies themselves often say that they attend exhibitions in order to keep up with competitors or to put forward the 'confident' image necessary in order to reassure shareholders, investors or customers.

Real advantages accrue from attendance at exhibitions, however. Sales are the ultimate purpose of exhibitions but they are not immediately available within the context of the exhibition. Exhibitions involve competition for the attention of visitors and this is direct contact with customers. Direct selling opportunities are nevertheless very limited here.

In summary, then, exhibitions offer a prime opportunity for launching new products or services and for building up contacts with channel members or potential customers for such products.

Conferences and their Settings

Exhibitions are often frantic, but conferences tend to be more sedate and quiet. Conference formats are highly structured and the contacts/networking opportunities available at the exhibition are strictly limited in this setting. Conferences are not highly conducive to sales. Those involved in conferences do not enter into these events with the expectation of being sold a product and are likely to be highly resistant to sales approaches.

The real purpose of conferences is to position the expertise inherent in a business brand. Reputations are established in the conference arena; this is particularly important in the context of business to business marketing, for example.

Conferences are also covered within the media, albeit often within specialised media, and this can be an important aspect of the media relations programme, the company may be mounting.

The company involved will determine the real importance of the conference, of course. It is vitally important that the company should have a very clear idea of exactly with whom they wish to communicate by way of the conference and what kinds of messages they wish to convey.

By the nature of the event, contacts made at a conference will be much lower than the numbers contacted at an exhibition.

The Value of Seminars

Because prospects are 'captive' in the seminar environment, selling opportunities must be greater. The key to success, then, is getting these captive prospects into the mousetrap by putting on the right kind of event. The seminar must be concerned with a topic of genuine interest and value to the audience involved. Often guest speakers are well-known celebrities, who can bring in the public in question.

While the prospects for selling may be good, the number of prospects is definitely limited. Where small but powerful groups of buyers are concerned (for instance, those in industrial markets), the seminar is a very important opportunity indeed, and the expense and investment of effort involved in reaching a small number of people can be justified. However, seminars are of almost no value when it comes to mass markets, for fairly obvious reasons.

Benefits

The most striking benefit of all three types of occasion is the fact that they provide 'hands-on' experience and direct contact. Those with whom we seek to communicate can touch, see, smell, taste or try out a product or service. This obviously depends on the product, but covers everything from new types of food to industrial machines. When the products or systems are large, complex or difficult to set up in a potential customer's premises, these occasions allow customers to see and try them.

They also, of course, provide the opportunity for manufacturers to receive and evaluate customer reactions to product features – to gather positive and negative reactions and to identify possible sources of trouble at a preliminary stage. Where the performance of competitor products has changed, these occasions may provide the opportunity to pick up vital market intelligence permitting product modification, or spark some other change in the marketing mix, such as repositioning.

This illustrates again the close and symbiotic relationship between elements of the marketing mix often seen as analytically separate – marketing communication and intelligence gathering (part of marketing research). These often overlap and, in practice, form part of the same concrete activities.

In addition, of course, it is important to recognise that participation at exhibitions, conferences or seminars would, in itself, be of limited value were it not for an effective promotion and publicising of the event and the company's participation in it. Effective publicity here will maximise the benefit to be obtained from participation.

It is also important to formulate an effective strategy to attract prospects to the stand or display the company sets up. This links to other aspects of the communications mix, such as the use of direct mail (invitations to attend, for example) advertising (specialised journals, posters, etc.) or even dissemination of literature through sales visits or other activities. This is also a fertile area for the operation of the public relations department; company participation can provide good stories for appropriate media.

At the event, interpersonal skills come into their own. This is a specialist area in its own right, of course, and it cannot be taken for granted that just anyone can 'work the crowd' develop prospects or interact with key target institutions and individuals to the best effect. Gathering contacts and leads to be followed up afterwards is a central part of this sort of activity.

When those leads are being followed after the event, further expenditure and investment of resources and effort is essential. Those benefits gathered from the exhibition conference or seminar need to be exploited to the full, whether that should be contacts or publicity or reputational gain from the presentation of information.

Often, video recordings are made of the proceedings of such events; these can then be used as part of promotional material used in presentations or packs sent out to publicise the company or its products. Increasingly, these are made available to television as part of press releases.

BARKER'S WRITING TECHNOLOGIES

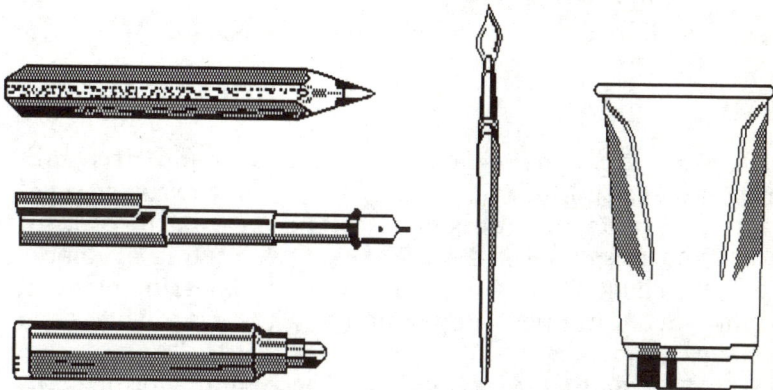

Barkers of the World – Unite!

Barker's pens are a bright light of quality in a world of cheap junk. Our products are better. Our marketing is better: the products are in the shops now – get out there and sell!

Betty Harrison's rousing speech climaxed the BWT conference with a fitting mood of aggression and enthusiasm. The new sales staff in the audience were infected by her vivacity and confidence and went away determined to make those sales targets.

Barker Writing Technologies (BWT) are one of the great success stories of the last decade. They have leapt ahead of the competition, but Harrison emphasised the need to stay ahead, and build on the excellent results of the last half-year.

Sales are successful

Mike Burnett, commercial manager said that for the 4th successive year, Barkers were ahead of budget, this year by more than 15 per cent. He also reported that, thanks to improvements in ordering procedures, products were getting to the retailer, and thus the customer, more quickly than ever before.

Rob Havering, divisional sales manager, national accounts, said that research findings indicated that the market overall was static, but that BWT's market share was still rising steadily. In a lively, well-illustrated presentation, he highlighted the ways the company had performed successfully, but also warned against complacency.

Creativity, creativity!!

Tim Hoggart, divisional sales manager, independent retail, uncorked an exciting new idea for BWT – a new artist's travel pack for Christmas, including an uncoloured card. The concept is that the card and artist's pack solves two buying problems with one purchase. This will also succeed in boosting sales in both the art supplies department and also the card department.

Business gifts aims to develop innovative plans for promoting customised products, and for new methods of distribution, according to Petra Wicks, divisional sales executive. A good example saw the recent links between BWT and Tomita, the Korean electronics giant, to produce a joint executive promotional pack to be sold and distributed under the Tomita badge.

Tony Hardy, manager of sales promotions, indicated that, in his view, staying ahead involved more than just maintaining market share or sales volumes, but aggressively attacking the strategies of competitors, since customers had little brand loyalty and comparison shopping was a matter of routine in this market.

Visibility in the stores was the key, he insisted. Although BWT were already leading at point-of-sale, as a result of special in-store promotional vehicles such as showcases, gondolas, display units, counter pads and 'spider' posters and badges. The sales promotion team would be ensuring that the company stayed that way by achieving maximum pull through of retail sales.

Advertising matters

Account director Karen McGregor, speaking on behalf of J Mathew Ogilvie, BWT's advertising agency, argued that the main direction for company advertising strategy would be towards development of roller ball pen sales, because of enormous growth in that market.

Expanding the strategy underlying the Autumn and Christmas poster and television campaigns. The campaigns

Christmas poster and television campaigns. The campaigns involve 'insects and bats' in order to build up interest in the roller ball colours and styles are part of the writing experience. The gold and platinum premium models would be featured in follow on campaigns, concentrating on the quality of the products but taking as a theme the 'Eldorado' of pens.

PR for BWT, Bert Bullion, PR consultant, offered an interesting account of the importance of press and publicity in support of marketing and promotion activity.

He showed how new products and promotional strategies are explained to retailers by placing new stories in magazines read by them.

For customers, PR finds ways of associating BWT and its products with prestige events like awards and competitions. It also looks at ways to persuade consumer magazines to carry features on BWT products as gift ideas.

Rock and Pop Musicplan representatives gave an interesting account of the way they had researched the rock and pop project and organised the BWT rock and pop disco at the Camden Palace in August. The girl rock group Kenickie have agreed to act as sponsors for the new line of elegant and colourful organiser products.

They explained that these pens would successfully launch BWT products into the youth market by linking the company and its products with the music, thus building up a relationship with lifetime pen users.

The new pens would be sold in record shops too and a special edition Kenickie pen will be given away to a limited number of purchasers of their new single *Writing the Future.*

Congratulations

Betty Harrison wound up the conference on a high note, congratulating the sales team on a fine performance. The marketing research was encouraging, but it must be passed on to the retailers, she insisted.

The joint venture with Tomita would spread BWT distribution and the 'art card' was a promising innovation, with heavy sales and a full order book. Marketing Services were achieving good 'pull through' of products by helping store promotions. This team alone was larger than the sales forces of competitors.

"Let's stay ahead," Betty Harrison said, "and grab every opportunity that arises." The conference ended as it had begun, on a high note.

6.1 *Why do BWT organise an annual sales conference?*

6.2. *What is a static market? What problems is this likely to cause BWT?*

6.3. *What are the main steps being taken by BWT to address their marketing problems?*

6.4. *Describe the main functions of conferences. How far does the BWT conference succeed in meeting these objectives?*

6.5. *What does the sales conference indicate about the promotional mix being used?*

6.6. *What would you change in the organisation of this company's marketing communications?*

7

MERCHANDISING AND PACKAGING

What is Merchandising? Why do it?

Merchandising refers to those techniques of communicating with the customer occurring at the point-of-sale (POS). It has only recently resumed its rightful place as a key tool in the marketing communications toolbox. For many years, merchandising was relegated to a marginal role and was employed in a limited number of settings, particularly what used to be called 'impulse purchases' within retail environments. It is now being used in every type of marketing.

Merchandising is concerned with the key moment in the marketing process — the final decision of purchase at the point-of-sale. This is becoming more and more important because shopping is now seen as a leisure activity and consumers are expecting more from the environments where goods are being retailed. Decisions are increasingly made inside the store and depend on messages and information available when the customer is actually standing in front of the product.

Tools for Merchandising

The tools used for merchandising include a wide range of the different features of the point-of-sale environment, which goes all the way from fundamental features of store design and layout, the range of goods available and the environment itself (music, lighting, etc.) up to a huge range of ways messages and information can be made available to the consumer. These include:

- leaflets;
- stickers;
- posters;
- display cards and special promotional units;
- bins;
- special promotional events and stalls;
- electronic display systems;
- shelving:
- space;

- positioning;
- sampling opportunities;
- window space.

Merchandising Factors: Techniques and Objectives

Each of these merchandising tools can contribute to the achievement of overall marketing communications objectives. These objectives, or areas of concern, usually fall into the following broad categories.

Store Image

The image of a store is partly determined by subconsciously perceived cues forming coherent patterns in the mind of the customer. The space available, the tidiness of the shelves, the number, range and types of goods, the noise level, the appearance and demeanour of staff, the effects of design features, etc. are all cues contributing to the formation of an overall pattern in the mind of the consumer.

Store Layout

This influences the ways consumers move around in the retail environment (traffic flow) and, therefore, the messages, products and areas to which they are exposed, the order, duration of exposure, etc. This can be crucial for successful marketing communications. Recent research has shown that identification and location of linked purchases by key groups is crucial in maximising consumer spend.

Merchandise Ranges

Locating fruit or perfume at the entrance of the store promotes powerful images of freshness and wholesomeness promoting consumer feelings of confidence and well-being. Impulse products are carefully located to maximise returns. This sometimes needs careful thought. Positioning confectionery at children's eye level close to the checkout used to be commonplace, but research revealed high levels of resentment amongst harassed parents who quickly saw through the marketing psychology involved. More socially responsible merchandise location has proven more profitable in terms of good image and friendly customer relations.

Diagram 7.1: Psychological Factors in Retail Design Context

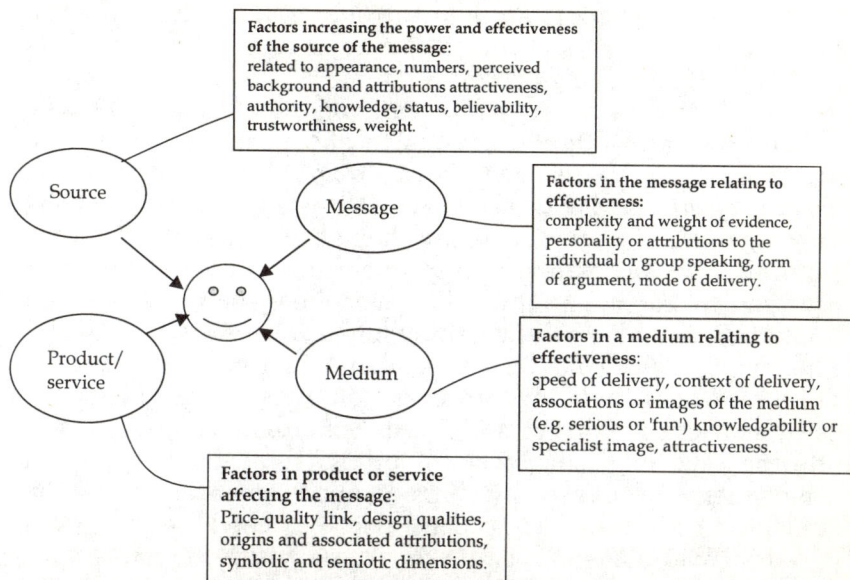

Factors increasing the power and effectiveness of the source of the message:
related to appearance, numbers, perceived background and attributions attractiveness, authority, knowledge, status, believability, trustworthiness, weight.

Source

Message

Factors in the message relating to effectiveness:
complexity and weight of evidence, personality or attributions to the individual or group speaking, form of argument, mode of delivery.

Product/ service

Medium

Factors in a medium relating to effectiveness:
speed of delivery, context of delivery, associations or images of the medium (e.g. serious or 'fun') knowledgability or specialist image, attractiveness.

Factors in product or service affecting the message:
Price-quality link, design qualities, origins and associated attributions, symbolic and semiotic dimensions.

Colour Arrangements on the Shelves

Gaining attention on the shelves is a perennial problem for merchandisers. Colour contrasts, surprisingly, are not necessarily desirable in this respect. Products very often have to stick to the conventions and the symbolic associations for certain product areas. For example, some foods would be adversely affected by the use of inappropriate colours in the packaging; similarly, when manufacturers wish to stress a particular product attribute, or stay in harmony with the overall communication objective by stressing, for example quality or exclusivity, then certain colours are almost unavoidable. Often, colours are 'blocked' on the shelves and arrangements tend to 'lead' the eye of the consumer towards a particular product or brand being emphasised. The allocation of shelf space is also critical. Computer software is now used to calculate optimum mixes.

POS Displays and Retail Sales Promotions

Retailers are now determined to maximise the yield per square metre of their store, which means that every available opportunity is taken to put on displays, sampling points, bins selling out of date, discontinued or slow moving goods at discounted prices. These displays may also be rented out to goods manufacturers, but it is essential that the ways this space is used should complement the advertising and publicity carried on in the same store or in related stores carrying the product lines. Various other techniques may be employed as part of merchandising activity.

Sound and music systems can also be used to convey information and offer directions to shoppers, to modify the atmosphere so as to slow down or speed up traffic flows. *Smells, scents and fragrances* are also used to change moods and buying behaviour. Research has shown that appropriate smells can make customers stay longer in front of displays and counters; it has been found that attitudes, such as trust and relaxation can also be affected by low levels of certain scents. The smell of baking bread is also a potent technique in promoting the sale of groceries or just as a means of establishing the correct ambience. Some new companies are offering special packages to promote specific types of atmosphere produced by introducing aromatics into the ventilation system. This can also be used to suppress potentially unpleasant odours occurring within the store.

Does it Work? Measuring Effectiveness

With the introduction of electronic point-of-sale (EPOS), which measures and records sales and other data using bar scanning equipment almost instantaneously, the effect on sales of specific measures or modifications in the merchandising/promotional mix being used can be measured with relative precision. Centralised data storage and ready access to computers to analyse this kind of data means that effects across a number of outlets can be measured very effectively.

In addition, there are a number of other techniques that can be used to measure the intended communications effects, e.g. remote equipment can monitor the length of time spent by customers in front of a display. Special equipment can also be used in order to monitor the ways customers scan the messages on particular displays.

Packaging

More than a Container

The packaging of a product is an integral part of advertising communication, as it functions effectively as an advertisement for the product at the point-of-sale. The main aspects of the package are technical design and surface design (the words and graphics printed on the package). Clearly, well-designed packaging will communicate important information to the potential consumer effectively and will also accomplish important image building, by reinforcing the qualities important for the 'selling proposition'.

FOUR MAIN FACTORS INVOLVED IN SURFACE DESIGN

1. Functionality (aspects of usage – storage, returns, visible contents, spoilage, resealing).
2. Shelf visibility.
3. Content communication.
4. Psychological connotations.

It has been said that packaging functions as a 'silent salesman', communicating the promotional message via the packaging used.

The pack can help customers by bringing the brand to their attention, highlighting the unique selling point (USP), offering information about the composition and characteristics of the product, the ways it can be used and related attributes of the product. Image characteristics too are conveyed in the design, colouring, shape, materials and information making up the package.

This adds value to the product and also improves the physical characteristics of the product by protecting and maintaining it (e.g. keeping food fresh). When the product is on the shelf, good packaging will make the product more distinctive and attractive and will also serve to advertise the product, essentially for free.

Recently, packaging has become an environmentally sensitive issue. Many manufacturers are now making this into a marketing benefit by espousing 'green' values in the kinds of packaging they use.

Basic Functions

Packaging should fulfil three basic functions.

1. **To protect** (serve as a container) each package may need to be transported, often in stacks with large numbers of others. Sometimes, the contents need to be kept away from the user (e.g. bleach, medicines).

Packages also serve as an indicator of purity or safety (e.g. they would indicate whether a product had been tampered with or used).

2.   **To provide a convenient vessel** (for pouring, serving, stacking, consuming, etc.). The right container will have a definite role to play in making the product more useable in many ways. This can be a very tangible product advantage.

3.   **To communicate in all the ways mentioned above**. However, it is worth commenting that these cannot be neatly separated off. Functionality in the above mentioned ways can be, in itself, an indicator of good design and an indicator of good quality. Being, for instance, in good condition as a result of strong and effective packaging will make the product more attractive and, consequently, more saleable.

Although one function may well be prioritised (out of necessity, usually) in virtually all designs, there is some degree of trade off between these different features. In some cases, it is necessary to make fine judgements about the cost of having very strong, or very high-grade, packaging and the benefits it brings. Packaging is a cost, like all others in business, should be carefully considered alongside the potential benefits expenditure in this area is actually bringing.

The Value of Tradition

While a recognised and respected packaging design is a potentially vital element in maintaining the market share a company enjoys, the marketplace (and the competition) are likely to change. A new generation of consumers represents the challenge to succeed again and again for long-established brands. It is therefore inevitable that it will be necessary, at some point, to consider the need for changing the packaging. Customers, even long-term, loyal ones, change: they become more affluent, more conservative, more conservationist, more interested in modern or exotic pastimes, more exposed to other cultures and new experiences through holidays or travel related to work, etc. As a consequence, they will develop new tastes, want something else from the products they buy. They may have bought food to enjoy and to fill them up when younger, but not they want health, animal rights and to save the environment. Products taking account of these aspirations will probably succeed; those who refuse to change may find their loyal customer base is shrinking.

Sometimes changes can be subtle but telling. 'Traditional' lettering, designed under the influence of art nouveau lithography, or what was then 'futuristic' lettering practices, may be subtly updated to give a more contemporary feel but retain the (still valuable) link with the successful and familiar packaging design of the 'old' product.

Packs and Brands

Family branding strategies mean that for many companies, a corporate name, logo and packaging style can be happily used across a complete portfolio of related products. Here, the strength of the brand name is so powerful that it can add great value to all the products within its ambit, even when they are relatively new to the marketplace. This may well produce trial purchases and the transfer of 'added value' from a well-established group.

'*Fighting brands*' also has its advantages. Here, the company is freer to move from one area to another and to allow individual brands to stand on their own. If they work, then all well and good – although there is such a high turnover of companies in what are increasingly fluid and competitive global markets that life expectancy for all but the very biggest brands must be highly questionable. If it does not do well, then no damage results for the parent company.

Communicating via the Packaging

The messages sent out by the pack about the characteristics, personality and image of the company involved are only part of its communications functions. The pack must also:

- gain the attention of the shopper;
- deliver a persuasive promise to the browsing customer;
- promote brand image and engage the customer;
- build loyalty to the brand with an attractive, convenient, distinctive, easy to use pack design;
- provide important usage information;
- provide important safety information.

The pack also serves as a complement to other marketing communication activities, e.g. it can serve as a 'trigger' re-activating memories of advertising messages spelled out in posters or television advertisements. A 'pack shot' (close up of the packaging) is standard in many advertisements and where the brand is long-established and dominant in a market, it will often serve as a 'trigger' above all else and concentrate on distinctiveness and the ability of its design to be recognised.

Design and Communication

Figure 7.2: The Packaging Design Process

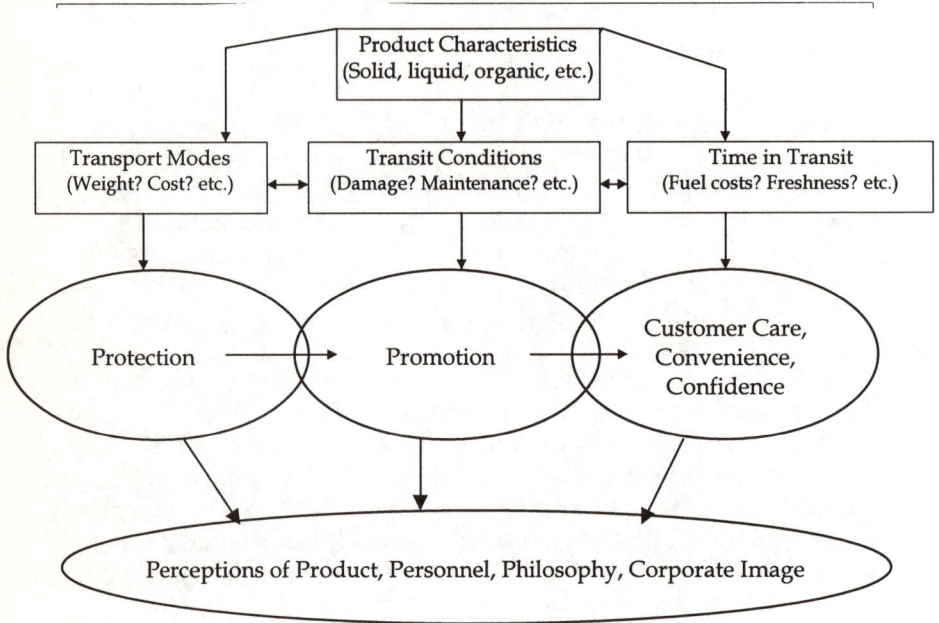

```
                    ┌─────────────────────────┐
                    │  Product Characteristics │
                    │ (Solid, liquid, organic, etc.) │
                    └─────────────────────────┘
   ┌──────────────────┐   ┌──────────────────┐   ┌──────────────────┐
   │ Transport Modes  │◄─►│ Transit Conditions │◄─►│  Time in Transit │
   │ (Weight? Cost? etc.) │ │ (Damage? Maintenance? etc.) │ │ (Fuel costs? Freshness? etc.) │
   └──────────────────┘   └──────────────────┘   └──────────────────┘

      ( Protection ) ──► ( Promotion ) ──► ( Customer Care,
                                              Convenience,
                                              Confidence )

   ( Perceptions of Product, Personnel, Philosophy, Corporate Image )
```

The main aspects of design – shape, size, colour, graphics, materials and smell – can each be used to achieve communication objectives. There are good psychological reasons to believe that within a particular culture, broadly similar associations are built into particular design features. Designers can expect to generate broadly similar reactions and associations when they apply particular shapes, colours, etc. in order to generate a particular 'brand value' such as 'love', 'quality' or 'efficiency'. Shape also provides a number of aesthetic satisfactions, such as ease or pleasure in handling or constitutes an effective way of delivering the product (e.g. squeezable bottles). The shape can also be the main element that is recognised – some drinks bottles (e.g. Coca-Cola) or dispensers (e.g. Jif lemon) are extremely recognisable.

Size is used to communicate a number of things. Products aimed at family purchasing (e.g. breakfast cereals) are targeting particular market segments and will not be bought by other groups. By offering sizes to cater for much lower volumes of consumption, the 'singles' market can be targeted. This is focused on practical issues, by and large. *Colour*, by contrast, is focused on emotional as well as physical dimensions. Colour can make a pack more recognisable and grab attention, but also makes an emotional appeal and is associated with states of excitation. Colours also have meaning – white is used to suggest purity, green to suggest naturalness and freshness, etc. The colours and design used in packaging have a direct influence on the ways consumers perceive the attributes of the product.

'Biarritz' chocolates, for example, were a repackaging exercise using exactly the same assortment as a long-established, moribund brand. Tests revealed that consumers perceived the taste of the repackaged chocolates to be "young, new and exciting". Other tests with food, detergents and so on reveal similar effects. It is important to remember, however, that the cultural differences exist and the meaning of, and preference for, particular kinds of colours, so that the same effects may not occur when a product is marketed in another country. Similarly, graphics can be used to create and reinforce brand values and to achieve 're-cognisability'. Images and lettering used both convey literal information and also create an impression or a 'mood'.

Packaging is also part of the environment (e.g. food used in the kitchen) and it is often important to think about the setting where the package will be used and kept. Again, of course, packaging can be part of the satisfaction a customer derives. Young drinkers, it has been found, derive important satisfactions from the use of 'stylish' cans or bottles, essentially functioning as a 'fashion accessory'. This is known in the drinks industry as 'badge drinking'.

This use of graphics commonly aims to create a mood or reflect the kind of values in lifestyle towards which the consumer aspires, for example 'country living' or 'success'. This is also true of the materials used (quality can be conveyed by using prestigious materials, such as glass or 'real wood'; similarly, value is conveyed by using cardboard or plastic). This can also serve as an indicator of the type of consumer for which the product is intended – children's snack food packaging, for example, is more likely to involve paper or cellophane. It is important, again, to recognise cultural variations. Many countries have a much lower usage of packaging materials than the UK or attach much greater significance to the use of particular kinds of materials (e.g. the importance of biodegradability or using natural materials).

SPORTIPLAST: THE ACTION TREATMENT

Medigro, the medical accessories giant, has announced a major new product for the fast-growing, sports medicine market with a brand new product. The *Sportipast Action Pack* aims to provide amateurs and professionals alike with a reasonably priced, injury prevention and treatment product in a compact, convenient form the packaging is a major feature of the new product. A handy, durable, light plastic drum is designed to fit into the sports bag without any fuss and to provide everything needed to cope with common sports injuries, such as blisters, abrasions and sprains. The long-lasting pack is intended to retail for less than £5.

The pack will contain enough materials to last for at least three months and will include zinc-oxide strapping, anchor dressings, antiseptic wipes, wound dressings, a crepe bandage and a medium lint dressing. The launch of the new product is being accompanied by a substantial advertising campaign and a programme of promotion among sports clubs and organisations. The new pack, intended for individual players not previously catered for by this kind of product, will complete the range of products offered by the Medigro group. This product follows the launch of *Teamdoc*, the product intended to cater for sports teams and clubs, as well as schools, the same kind of facility.

Medical experts and sports specialists were involved in the design of the case and its contents. All can be replenished individually from corner chemists and supermarket pharmacies. According to reports in the sports literature, Medigro products are the most well regarded and widely used in the field, by both professionals and amateurs.

Medigro themselves have mounted a public information

programme to educate players on the prevention and treatment of common sports injuries. This is also intended to publicise the availability and usage of Medigro products. The programme includes a sport safety video, available free of charge to clubs, schools and organisations and, targeted at coaches and sponsorship of football, "Coaching and Physio Injury Guide" courses, and 'preventing injury' pamphlets, directed at rugby players.

Tennis is also provided for with sponsorship of a number of mobile, first-aid stations for official LTA events. Medigro has been adopted as official supplier of medical first aid equipment by the leading organisations in football, rugby league, squash, badminton, fencing and basketball.

7.1. *What were the main objectives for designers in creating this pack? Indicate what alternatives might have been considered and the reasons for accepting or rejecting them.*

7.2 *Describe the typical stages of the packaging design process and relate them to this case, making appropriate assumptions.*

7.3 *Draw what you think this pack will look like, indicating the main features. Specify the colours and logos you would use, the information you would include on the display and the special features the pack should have, in view of its intended use.*

7.4 *Repeat the above process for a pack intended for use by older people.*

7.5 *Assess the advantages and disadvantages of this packaging for customer and company.*

7.6 *Discuss ways in which other aspects of the promotional and communications mix could be used to reinforce the special features of this newly launched product*

7.7 *What did these designers take into account when designing the new pack for Sportiplast?*

7.8 *What are the marketing communications issues that must be taken into account when designing this pack?*

MELDRITE: WRAPPING UP THE MARKET

Talk about coals to Newcastle! Thanks to a new wonder wrapping, a new food company is cleaning up in EC markets, selling garlic bread to the French!

Meldrite, produced by the chemical giant LDL, is a wonderful, new, transparent wrapping with none of the undesirable qualities of the older materials (such as leaching chemicals into oil-based foods) and manages to create and sustain an airtight sterile environment. This improves a product's keeping qualities while keeping it juicy and fresh whenever it is removed.

French Kitchen, the baking and catering chain, has used the new product to such good effect, that it turned to LDL's plastics and petrochemicals division when it sought to fill the niche market for rolls and sandwiches in the catering and snack sector. It had spotted a gap in the market for premium-priced, high-quality snacks suitable for the traveller and business representative and, given the available expertise within the company (as well as trends towards more exotic cuisine fuelled by foreign holidays), garlic bread-based snacks seemed a logical move.

The company also recognised the importance of ready-made sandwich snacks for the busy family too, so they needed a packaging material to survive and function in the environment of the chill cabinet in the supermarket (where 95 per cent of all household provisions are bought, including sandwiches in this time-famine era).

Chilled foods have been one of the fastest growing sectors of the UK food market in the past ten years and, alongside this, we have seen a huge upsurge of interest in more savoury foods. Those featuring the flavours for which British holidays in the sun have given us a greater appreciation – olive oil, pasta and, of course, garlic – are particularly important. Garlic bread, as a standard item for the proposed sandwich range, could complement the existing range of French Kitchen specialities also including continental favourites, such as pizza and pot au feu. This heavy flavouring, however, poses its own problems.

> *"We realised straightaway that we had very exacting packaging specification," says marketing and sales director, Janet Porterhouse, "and that we also wanted this product to do quite a few things apart from just keep the bread fresh. The product needed something to keep it fresh, but it also had to let people see the freshness of the bread and the colours of the filling. Our research tells us these are key factors in attracting the 'grazing' shopper who wants a delicious snack. We also needed something to look good in the cook chill cabinet, but which could also stand being heated in the oven or microwave without reacting badly and contaminating the food. It needed to be cookable in a conventional oven but had to keep the flavour away from other items in the oven. One of the problems with garlic flavoured products in the past has been the tendency for the flavour to 'leak' over into other parts of the display cabinet or else to other dishes and ingredients being cooked in the same oven."*

Meldrite was rigorously tested alongside a number of other potential materials before being selected. As an added bonus, the product also takes graphic inks without being affected in any way, enabling the company to incorporate advertising messages – something never before possible with this kind of packaging.

> *"We are delighted," said Ms Porterhouse, "we believe that this packaging has been a key factor in the success of the product, because it provides us with key competitive advantages. These can be passed on to the retailer in the form of better quality and longer shelf life and the customer in the form of*

*added convenience and superior flavour. These
products are now our fastest selling item, not just in
this country, but on the continent too."*

Amazing though it sounds, this company now exports garlic
bread back to France and a major reason is the packaging
itself, which is not available to producers in that country.
LDL's Gavin Meister commented:

*Meldrite was developed specifically for the French
Kitchen range. Its ability to be heat-sealed helps
maintain the product's freshness, clarity and
natural sparkle. All of these natural features of a
food product are its premier selling points with
customers and if the packaging helps get them
across, it has to be a big plus for the marketing mix.
On a practical level, the product also performs;
keeping odours and flavour in the same container,
at extremes of temperature is a real benefit and
customers know about that because it's written on
the packaging.*

If the sales in France are anything to go by, this has been
acknowledged by a nation of gourmets. Watch out though –
the snails will be coming next.

7.9. *Why was Meldrite chosen as the packaging
material for this product?*

7.10 *What aspects of the product are being communicated by the use of this packaging material?*

7.11 *Devise an appropriate name and logo for this
range of products. Indicate what messages you
would put on the packaging and say why they
would be there.*

7.12 *What parts of the marketing communications mix
might usefully complement this technological
breakthrough in packaging? Indicate what communications objectives you think they should have.*

8
PLANNING, IMPLEMENTING AND CONTROLLING MARKETING COMMUNICATIONS

Planning

The first stage of this process undoubtedly requires the development of an outline plan, which begins to lay down the priorities the company ought to be pursuing. The outline plan will lay down the kinds of built-in reviews that ought to take place before objectives can be properly set and then to sketch in the kinds of strategies, tactics and resources. An outline plan would probably contain the following elements.

- **A review of the present situation**, including a breakdown of the company itself, its products and the market within which it operates.
- **A statement of objectives**, broken down into short, medium and long-term. Also by type (corporate, marketing, marketing communication, etc.).
- **An outline of strategies** that will be followed to achieve the objectives – specifying the communications and marketing strategies to be put in place.
- **An outline of the tactics** that might be employed – specifying what will be done, in what manner and when, etc.
- **A specification of target markets and a description of market segments**, broken down in terms of behavioural, attitudinal and usage characteristics or whatever segmentation variables are deemed appropriate.
- **An outline of manpower required**, relating the types of skilled workers needed for the kind of tasks required.
- **A breakdown of the budget**, relating in detail to the activities involved and to the expected returns in terms of increased sales, market share, etc.
- **An outline of the schedule involved**, laying down time horizons and a timetable for all the major objectives and stages of the marketing process.

Details of the monitoring and measurement processes will indicate when, and if, objectives are being met. This is essential to enable those in charge of the marketing process to identify which parts of the programme are working. Thus the experience is also a learning curve and potentially expensive mistakes can be ironed out for future reference.

Situation Analysis

The best way to build up a systematic picture of the situation from which the company is starting in the development of its

Figure 8.1: The Fact Book

Outline

A. *Product facts*
1. General product class, how it is manufactured, raw materials, etc.
2. Company brand history.
3. Competitive products and characteristics.

B. *Market facts*
1. Distribution, methods, coverage by region, store size, package size, etc.
2. Sales history for product class.
3. Sales history for brand by region, package size, etc.
4. Competitive sales and brand shares by region, etc.
5. Consumer uses/habits, units of purchase, fre-   quency of use, loyalty.
6. Consumer attitudes, motivations, preferences.
7. Industry practices and restrictions, pricing, sales promotions, etc.
8. Pricing history, dealer margins, discount structure, etc.

C. *Gross profit history*

D. *Advertising history*
1. Expenditures, copy approaches, media strategy, etc.

E. *Sales promotion history*

F. *Merchandising history*

G. *History of sales procedures*

H. *Packaging history*

I. *Review of previous marketing plans*

---

plan is to build up a 'fact book'. This is the recommendation made in the planning programme laid out in the Eldridge marketing plan. A fact book involves a gathering of all relevant facts covering the sections outlined in Figure 8.1.

This is the essential basis for implementing the Eldridge marketing plan, which is a typical format for marketing planning. It incorporates the elements highlighted in Figure 8.2.

Figure 8.2: The Eldridge Marketing Plan

1. A statement of facts, summarised from the fact book.
2. A product philosophy.
3. Problems and opportunities involved in the situational context.
4. Objectives and basic strategy.
5. Plan of action.
6. Marketing appropriation.
7. Sales and profit forecasts.
8. Summary of plan.

Objectives

As far as objectives are concerned, a number of issues need addressing if the marketing communications plan is to succeed.

* At which consumer groups should these messages be directed?
* What information will these consumer groups seek from our communications when deciding whether or not to buy?
* What objectives should be set in order to communicate effectively with these groups?
* How much will it cost to achieve these objectives? What size should the total budget be?
* How should this total budget be apportioned among the various marketing communication activities available?
* How much responsibility is to be assumed by the manufacturers and by the channel intermediaries?
* How might the effectiveness of the campaign be evaluated and controlled?

Addressing these issues is a key aspect of integrated communication marketing. This involves setting *communication objectives*.

Marketing communication objectives, in themselves, are specific and short-term. They must be in line with overall product strategy. Their main purpose is to co-ordinate and focus the work of individual departments. It can, for example, specify the aims of copywriting, personal selling advertising and below-the-line promotional activities. Setting clear, precise and measurable objectives helps to integrate marketing communications with the marketing activities. It also improves liaison with external agencies and permits the determination of communications budgets and appropriations. It also secures appraisal of the plans by top management. Objectives also measure the results of communication.

According to research by Britt and Majaro, most organisations fail to specify objectives clearly enough, with the consequence that often the tactics used will tend to be out of sync with each other or even work in opposite ways.

Communication Objectives

There are two main types of communication objectives – those addressed to consumers, or potential consumers, and those addressed to those within the trade. These have quite different purposes, and the kinds of objectives they are pursuing are consequently likely to be quite different.

1. *Consumer communications* aim to:
   a) inform about new products;
   b) correct misconceptions about a product;
   c) increase frequency of usage;
   d) remind;
   e) present special offers;
   f) educate consumers in how to use a product;
   g) build up an image for the product/company;
   h) build up consumer loyalty.
2. *Trade communications* seek to:
   a) provide information;
   b) inform about promotional programmes;
   c) present special trade offers;
   d) avoid stockpiling;
   e) educate the trade on product usage;
   f) build patronage motives.

Note the importance of the following.

1. Non-marketer dominated information sources. Contradictory information may be carried here and may frustrate communications objectives.

2.   The need to identify and satisfy the target audience interests in information. Are there gaps in the communications plan, which means the consumers are not getting the information they want?

3.   The need to maximise expenditure so that the marginal cost of disseminating the information does not exceed the marginal revenue brought about.

4.   The need to identify the extent to which the information needs of the buying prospects can be resolved by promotional elements of the marketing mix, or by non-promotional elements, and to work out a resolution of the balance between these elements.

Corporate Strategies

The communication objectives need to be pursued in a systematic manner. In a corporate strategy, the long-range goals, policies and objectives of the company are specified, this would include, for example, the product assortment or range to be provided by the company, the profitability level to be sought, the growth rate, the corporate image and funding.

Corporate strategy directly influences marketing strategy and sets optimum elements of the marketing mix. This, in turn, determines the form of promotional activity and which marketing communications are developed and used.

The type of marketing strategy used will have a direct bearing on the kinds of marketing communications produced. *Branding strategy*, for example, will be concerned to promulgate and transmit the personality and attributes of the brand to the target group. This will involve:

a) **product modification strategy**: the necessity to re-position the product in terms of attributes meeting identified consumer needs. The communication strategy being followed here would aim to provide information about the modifications and to communicate the ways the product is to be differentiated from competitors;

b) **market segmentation strategy**: concerned with focusing on the needs of a specific market segment and messages should be formulated, and also channelled, through appropriate media and in forms to suit the ways in which media are used by the target group.

Advertising strategies may fall into a number of different camps. One way is to think of them as pursuing alternative types of corporate objective, for example:

- product differentiation versus brand differentiation strategy;
- market expansion strategy;
- brand positioning strategy.

All of these are based on empirical research. The marketing plan provides the basis for a creative strategy rationale, which dictates the form of advertising. The basic aspects of marketing communication planning involve a number of different stages.

First comes the *identification of the target audience*. This determines what the communication is trying to say and how the message is to be expressed. Second is *the creation of a specific message*, turning a purchase proposition into an advertising idea.

The *selection of media* to use in the communication process is based on communication objectives for the product. The main influences on this choice are:

- location and accessibility of prospects;
- socio-economic/psychographic   characteristics   of prospects;
- purchase frequency and usage;
- price;
- area sales performance relative to competition;
- distribution and sales plans;
- ideal creative requirements for the campaign;
- media costs;
- number of readers or views.

Media scheduling depends, in part, on the size of budget but is also affected by competitive activity, the suitability and effectiveness of medium ('reach'), the relative importance of coverage and frequency and the importance of influencing distributors.

Determining the advertising budget is the final stage and is influenced by the marketing objectives for the period, the types of advertising required, the selection of media and how often ads should appear. It is important to build in the means of checking the effectiveness of advertisements to allow for changes of strategy. The advertising budget can be decided by one of these methods:

- percentage of past sales;
- percentage of anticipated sales;
- competitive parity;
- task methods;
- 'all you can afford'.

Measuring communication effectiveness is an important aspect of the overall plan. This is difficult to measure in terms of sales because there are so many 'confounding factors', which can be misleading. For instance, sales may be depressed by factors totally beyond the control of the marketer (such as the weather, competitor activity or public 'scares') in spite of communications working well and succeeding in the communication objectives they have been set up to achieve. It is consequently more usual to attempt to measure effective-ness in terms of communication goals.

Common methods of measuring this effectiveness include:

1.   **recall tests**: here consumers are asked about aspects of a particular advertisement they can recall. This may be based on either an 'unprompted' recall, or a 'prompted recall'. Unprompted recall merely asks which aspects of a company's advertising the test subject can remember. Prompted recall involves asking this question and others, after consumers have been exposed to advertising for the brand in question;
2.   **recognition tests**: these involve offering stimuli to the consumers in order to prompt recognition of product features and marketing messages.

The marketing plan develops a *product philosophy* along with a plan of action. Creative strategy is derived basically from a marketing plan. Creative implementation contains the following elements.

1.   Creative strategy rationale.
2.   Copy platform.

The *creative strategy rationale* is a document that summarises the thinking behind the proposed campaign. Its purpose is, first of all, to translate the strategy statement in the marketing plan into terms appropriate for the creative team. Secondly, it states what attributes and benefits will be stressed and what the characteristics of the marketing target will be. Thirdly, it also directs the efforts of writers, artists, filmmakers, producers, etc.

The *copy platform* states the central themes to be developed in the communications and also the claims to be made about the performance and qualities of the product. It also states the importance of each and assigns their overall place within the formulation of messages.

Principal elements in the copy platform include the following.

- **Principal theme/selling idea**: this is the main idea in the messages. It is sometimes referred to as the USP (unique selling point), the selling proposition or the product differentiation element.
- **'Mood'**: this is the 'atmosphere' to be developed within the advertising and so on. This would be stated as, for example, 'romantic', 'jolly', 'surreal' or 'serious'.
- **Expressions of product features**: this includes the key images or sequences focusing on the ways the principal theme or selling idea is concerned with a product feature. For example, the tread on a tyre being sold on the way it 'grips' the road and handles rain and snow.

Corporate Tactics

Tactics are concerned with the way in which the aims of the company's advertising strategies are achieved. For example, we may have relatively straightforward objectives but we need to specify the ways they are to be achieved, to look at the different types of methods which would help us to gain our objective and the ways these fit together.

1. **Creating awareness**, for example, is generally the first stage following the launch (or re-launch) of a product. It is important to remember that developing a communica-tions programme is sequential and will move on to other stages.
2. **Engendering favourable attitudes**: this is broadly the second phase and is followed by
3. **Generating action (purchase)**.

Each of these stages will require its own specific set of methods and techniques but these will have to be deployed bearing in mind the fact that there will be other stages in the sequence.

Media Characteristics

In developing a communications strategy, it is essential to be aware of the nature of the media being using. This is a vital element in working out the ways in which strategic objectives can be achieved through tactical means. You need to consider the positive and negative dimensions of the media you are using and calculate carefully what balance of these you can afford for the campaign you are undertaking.

Basic steps in media planning are as follows.

1. Define the target market reached by the media.
2. Define the product or service to be advertised.
3. Define the distribution system.
4. Define the purpose of the campaign.
5. Appraise competitor activity.
6. Assess media research.
7. Select the class of medium.
8. Select the media group.
9. Select the sub-group in the chosen medium.
10. Decide on the frequency, coverage and size in relation to the costs and appropriation available.

Tactics and the Copy Platform

As we have said, this summarises the message strategy decisions behind an individual advertisement. It combines advertising decisions (problem, objective targeting) with sales strategy.

Diagram 8.3: The Creative Platform

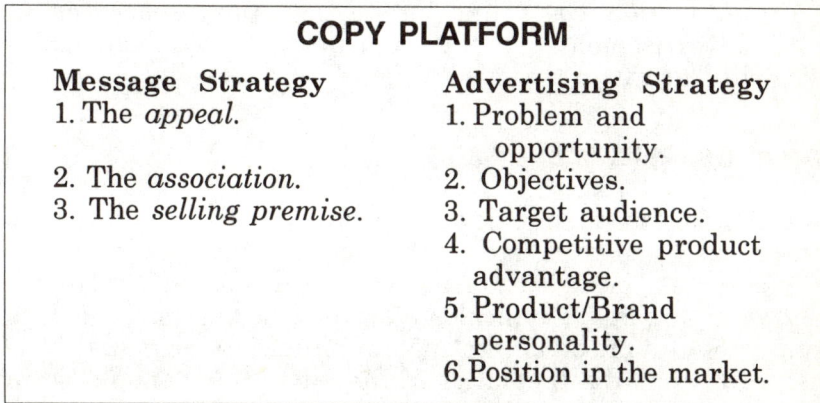

COPY PLATFORM	
Message Strategy	**Advertising Strategy**
1. The *appeal*.	1. Problem and opportunity.
2. The *association*.	2. Objectives.
3. The *selling premise*.	3. Target audience.
	4. Competitive product advantage.
	5. Product/Brand personality.
	6. Position in the market.

Usually a simple document, although varied from agency to agency, the creative platform sets a series of markers for the efforts of marketing and design professionals to work towards.

Advertising and personal selling are not, contrary to popular belief, the only tools available to the marketer. Other ways of disseminating information include the other communications techniques we have discussed. These include:

• publicity;

- public relations;
- short and long-term sales promotions;
- packaging.

The methods employed depend on various factors.

- Where are decisions taken by consumers? (At home? In a store? etc.)
- The nature of the product, simple (e.g. convenience goods using mass advertising) or complex (which may involve personal selling).
- The kind of information involved.
- Product strategy, content of communications, the target audience, etc.

There are three essential steps to be considered.

1. **Determining the content of the message**. We are aiming for consistency of information from various sources
2. **Presenting the message**, identifying a central idea and the way in which it is to be expressed and creating the advertisements and sales approach
3. **Determining how the communications effort will be produced**, for example, estimates of the production costs and production time schedules of advertisements, point of sale material and sales literature.

Advertising Themes

Advertising themes are the constant subject of creative work and are usually the specialised province of professionals brought in from various agencies. Figure 8.4 shows examples of typical advertising themes used in the imp-lementation of marketing communications plans. It is essential that the thematics of the advertising should be in accordance with the objectives laid out in the plans at both a corporate level and as expressed in the specific objectives of the marketing plan.

The Role of Marketing Communications in Industrial Marketing

The role of marketing communications in industrial marketing is different from that in mass-market situations and so the same criteria cannot be applied to the ways in which it

Figure 8.4: Advertising Themes (after Sternthal & Craig)

THEME (Example)	EXPLANATION
A. Product or Service-related	
1. Product or service features described "Less bovver than a hover".	Dominant features.
2. Product or service cited competitor's disadvantages.	Competitive advantage.
3. Product/service prices feature.	Price a dominant.
4. Product/service news dominant.	News/information.
5. Product/service popularity.	Size of market detailed.
6. Generic "Give em seafish".	Primary demand sought.
B. Consumer-related	
1. Consumer uses in product/service ads,	Uses explained, recipes, etc.
2. Savings through uses	Cost benefits of p/s shown lower gas bill with double glazing
3. Consumer self-enhancement dental fixative	Emphasis on how p/s helps consumer improve
4. Fear displayed	Threatening situations American Express – risks of cash carrying
5. Subsidised p/s trials "money off" intro purchases	Incentives to encourage p/s
C. Non-Consumer/Non-Product/Service-related	
1. Corporate citizenship BP – British technology	Favourable image sought
2. Investor advertising solicitations	Growth, profits and "business potential described to attract investors"

functions. It is much more likely to be concerned with:

- awareness building;
- comprehension building;
- efficient reminding;
- lead generation;
- legitimation;
- reassurance.

This is, of course, because industrial markets are much smaller and more specialised than mass markets and therefore the role of personal selling, and the development of longer term relations with clients, is of much greater importance.

Summary of the Planning Process

A number of specific steps are involved in planning a campaign, these include the following.

Step 1: Identifying the target audience. This involves the identification of relevant audience characteristics, these would focus on the social and psycho-social for consumer goods and services, in order to provide a basis for effective communications. For industrial goods, however, they would be commercial and economic.

Step 2: Specifying the promotional image. What are the bases for audience selectivity? Defining the objectives, the audience, etc. is of essential importance in terms of the functions of the campaign. This is the stage at which the types of appeal to be used are decided.

Step 3: Selecting the media. Media should be selected according to the target market, consumer characteristics, marketing objectives, etc.

Step 4: Scheduling the media.

Step 5: Setting the promotional budget.

Step 6: Measuring the success of advertising. Effective formulation and implementation of plans, however, cannot take place without good systematic foundations. Before the plan itself, we need to undertake an exhaustive *situation analysis*. This cannot in itself proceed unless we have also carried out a careful and thorough *product analysis*.

In short, the background or context within which the plan is being implemented must be thoroughly worked out. Prevailing *trends* need to be discovered and thoroughly understood before the campaign can proceed.

Objectives whether in *marketing* or *communications* must be established only with a thorough analysis of the setting in place. Only then can we begin to work out an effective strategy – deploying the tactics, marketing practice and the use of good creative personnel allows.

Market segmentation can only be worked out on the basis of good research and a full appreciation of who customers are likely to be and exactly those needs our product will aim to satisfy.

Personnel is also an important consideration. Depending on the nature of the techniques employed, differing skills will be required, sometimes in isolation, sometimes working in concert. These go all the way from creative teams working on advertising, to sales personnel building up long-term relationships with buying team personnel in industrial marketing.

Budgets the factors relevant to deciding the promotional allocation include:

a)   **the level of promotional spending in the target markets**; here, small companies take their cue from larger organisations;

b)   **the level of sales generated by promotional activity**;

c)   **the objectives sought** (objectives and task method). How much expenditure is necessary to achieve these objectives?;

d)   **the affordability of proposals** typically, after other costs centres have received their budgets, what is left over goes to promotion.

Each of these factors may form the basis for decisions about budget allocation but note, if sales are the deciding factor, the tendency is for falling sales to entail a falling budget (whereas the reverse should be the case, if we think about it for a moment).

In common practice, the task method, in which budgeting is related to the more specific forces influencing the decision making and transformation forces of the organisation, is widely supported.

Timescales

Any well-worked out plan must include the length of time available and the target deadlines for each of the stages of each activity involved in marketing communications. These would include proposals, concept development, testing the concepts to be deployed in the advertising and other communications strategies, including allowances for differences in the concepts to be deployed in each region, or each part of the world if this is an international campaign. If there is to be a movement through various levels or stages, it is important that this should be carefully phased and timed.

Monitoring and Measuring

This is essential, in order to detect:

- when things are working;
- when things are not working;
- what effects various measures have;
- when we have achieved our objectives.

If monitoring procedures are not in place, a plan cannot be implemented sensibly.

LOC-ALE! THERE'S NO TASTE LIKE HOME, SAYS MAJOR BREWER

Everyone likes to think that the beer in the local pub is better than anywhere else, but much of the time, local beers are actually brewed by the same company throughout the UK. One such is the major brewer, Whitebird. Through a series of acquisitions and mergers carried out over the years, Whitebird have acquired local names of great distinction in the brewing industry such as Nethereds Chastors and Blowers, tied to their local communities for more than a hundred years in some cases.

Whitebird is now an umbrella organisation incorporating some of the most revered names in regional brewing. The company offers customers one of the largest ranges of beers of any major brewer. The company markets more than twenty regional ales ranging from small, highly localised brands, such as Grantleys Yorkshire Bitter, to major regional brands, such as Valleys Bitter and Whitebird's Best Scotch. Many are cask conditioned, some brewery conditioned – it all depends on local taste, say the company, and the customer, in this case, always knows best!

According to brand manager Steven Dorfus, the volume markets lie, of course, with the big name brands, such as Whitebird's Best Scotch and Trojan Bitter. Regional preferences are a big factor, however, in many parts of the country and this needs to be taken into account as part of an effective overall strategy for marketing the Whitebird portfolio. Maintaining a range of local beers alongside the big sellers enables them to meet this demand – and give consumers a choice. These consumers, of course, do not stick to the same product continually, but certainly mix and change according to mood and circumstance. This is particularly true of younger consumers, who are far less brand loyal than the traditional beer drinker.

In any case, so-called regional brands are very significant sellers in their own right; Whitebird Scotch for instance, sells in very large amounts in the north east of Britain, growing at a time when the market for ale was generally sluggish. The importance of this brand for Whitebird overall is reflected in the intention to put a large amount of money into a campaign aiming to reinforce the success of this particular brand.

Whitebird Welsh Bitter is another example of a major regional brand whose success is being backed up by extensive television advertising. This backs up its regional identity according to the company.

Advertising the Chastor Brand in the Huddersfield area proved particularly successful, says Mr Dorfus.

> *Our advertising built directly on the strong local connection, and we were able to emphasise the idea of 'Hidderfield's Home Brew' connecting the brand to local history and personalities from the area.*

North western consumers are served by four main local brews. The local taste is for light and mild products and Hamlesbury Ales produce Whitebird Light to meet this preference; as the name suggests its a light beer but with a good flavour. Chastor's Light is another with a light but pronounced and distinctive flavour.

The Chastors beers are actually brewed in Salveston, with Best Mild and Best Bitter being available in both cask and bright versions, to cater for the modern and the more tradition-minded 'real ale' enthusiast.

The north east has five main brews. Local taste here is slightly wider, running from both cask conditioned and brewery conditioned formats. This is mostly produced at Sheffield's Whitebird Brewery.

Eden Moat brewery produces a wide range of beers, the most famous of which is Whitebird's Best Scotch, a massive seller locally and nationally. This is a full flavoured 'bright' beer appealing to the traditional palate of the established Scotch drinker. Eden Moat Ale, one of the traditional beers of the region has become one of the most popular cask conditioned bright beers in many other parts of the country.

Whitebird Ordinary is light, and specially brewed to meet the needs of the locals. Stockton Ale is a smooth, traditional ale suited to the palate of those in the south Durham area.

Brewing in Wales takes place at the Nagorn brewery and involves two main beers. Whitebird Welsh is a bitter produced to the tastes of the local market, while Whitebird Amber is a light mild brew again specific to the Welsh palate. Sam Strong's brew is slightly more full-flavoured, with a good body to the flavour and, although a minority taste, commands a good following in Wales.

The south west of England has taken Whitebird Game to its heart. This is a low gravity bitter specially developed for this market, and is coming to rival the long established Potter's IPA, also a significant presence in the Welsh market. Pale ales also sell well throughout the south, although Whitebird's Pale is brewed in the south west, near Cheltenham. Real Country Bitter is specifically brewed for the area surrounding Hampshire, Sussex and the New Forest. The portfolio for this area is completed by the high gravity traditional beer called Porter's Old Original, again a popular brand throughout the south of England, although original to the south west.

The massive markets in London and the south east are still served by the long established Gremlin's and Bletherhead's, and these remain some of the best selling beers in the country because of their presence on the huge London and home counties markets.

The original Bletherhead's Brewery in Buckinghamshire produces the only seasonal beer in the company's portfolio, Winter Prince. This is, as the name suggests, a premium cask conditioned beer, in the 1050+ range of specific gravity (this is the high-gravity range) but it is only available from October to April. This is a very unusual product, but with the de-regulation of the sector, it has become extremely popular as a guest beer, and as part of the portfolio offered by some of the new 'pub companies' managed public houses offering nothing but a rotation of guest beers from all over the country.

Bletherhead's bitter and SPA are also becoming more

ubiquitous throughout the UK, although their volume market remains in the south.

Gremlin's range remain highly popular locally but have so far not moved into the mainstream market. These are produced at Frodsham and comprise a light mild, Gremlins AK, and a cask conditioned bitter, Gremlin's Best.

8.1   *Why does Whitebird need to include local ales in its product portfolio?*

8.2   *What implications does this have for Whitebird's communications mix?*

8.3   *What are the advantages and disadvantages of this approach?*

8.4   *Analyse the issues facing a national co-ordinator for Whitebird's advertising. Identify the key issues the company needs to consider, and formulate an appropriate campaign mix. Write notes for the presentation you will give to regional brand managers at the annual Whitebird sales convention.*

8.5   *Design an advertising slogan makes a virtue of the strong regional presence of Whitebird brews. Indicate what it is intended to convey and why you consider this to be worth communicating to Whitebird customers.*

9
INTERNATIONAL AND GLOBAL MARKETING COMMUNICATIONS: GLOBAL MARKETS?

Much has been made of globalisation as a process and of the consequent homogeneity of consumer marketing in many different parts of the world. The 'MacDonaldisation' of world cultures has been much discussed and there is evidence to back-up this idea; many products appear in a great many different countries and we can find evidence to suggest that consumers in many different settings now share the same sorts of needs and desires.

The main factors in globalisation are:

- communication media;
- tourism;
- corporate growth;
- technologies of production;
- opening up of trade between countries;
- political change.

Cultural differences still matter, however, and can make the difference between success and failure for the marketers involved. The presence or absence of a product does not imply that consumers in different settings use or think about it in the same way; products may mean very different things to different groups of consumers.

According to Keegan, there are five main strategies for competing in global markets.

1. **Same product/Same communications** where need and use is the same.
2. **Same product/Different communication** where the needs or uses are different, but the product (physically) is the same, for example, bicycles are leisure goods in Britain or the US, but transport in many other parts of the world.
3. **Different product/Same communication** a different product according to local conditions but the same logo, for example, New Zealand Lamb products satisfying specific dietary requirements, such as halal slaughter.
4. **Different product/Different communications** where culture is the key differentiator.

5. **New product/New communication** the clockwork radio, for example.

Communications Strategies

The degree to which advertising can or should be standardised obviously depends upon the nature of the product and the particular setting where it is being marketed. There are four basic possibilities.

1. **Standardised and centralised advertising** means completely standardised advertising. Everything is controlled centrally.
2. **Decentralised and autocratic advertising** is the opposite, everything is decided at local level.
3. **Central strategies produced locally** allows a central determination of key areas, with local input and formulation of appropriate productions.
4. **Central formulation of strategy** with central and local production, here, for example, a 'master' advertisement is produced to which words and music can be added at the local level (for example, the case of Levi-Strauss advertising).

Figure 9.1: Appraisal of Advertising Standardisation

- Advantages.
- Consistency.
- Globalised market shares.
- Consistency.
- More cost-effective.
- More resource effective.
- Transfers skills.
- Ease of management.
- Disadvantages.
- Inhibits local creativity and input.
- Failure to exploit local conditions effectively.
- Dangers involved in cultural gaffes (see below).
- Failure to exploit local staff and to export skills.

Marketing Communications in an International Context

Even between neighbouring countries (such as France and Spain or Zimbabwe and South Africa) cultural differences can be very great. Marketing managers should always be aware of the importance of this "silent language", as Hall referred to it. The main aspects of cultural systems germane to marketing planning would cover the following areas.

Material Culture

This affects:

- **The level of demand**

   The lack of electricity will restrict the demand for electronic items. An American firm set out to launch a best selling cake mix in 1950s Japan on the basis of rising disposable income and increasing popularity for things Western – only to find that Japanese kitchens were not equipped with ovens to bake the product.

- **Quality and types of products demanded**

   Disposable income surely influences differences in the kinds of goods demanded. But note also the symbolic importance of particular goods to be used for exchange but more importantly for display (for example, the popularity of comparatively expensive Western cigarettes and sunglasses in communist China).

- **Functional/Usage characteristics**

   Demand for 'snack food' and the habit of 'grazing' has been stimulated in the UK by changes in the social roles of women and in the activities taking place within the home.

- **The nature of the products demanded**

   Menu meals are produced to help housewives prepare quality food when the time cannot be spared for shopping and cooking because many are now in full-time employment.

- **Social institutions**

   This relates to the social order, which gives a society its distinctive form and refers to the structures developed around particular aspects of the life experience (for example, the care and training of children or coping with conflict or suffering). The form of social institution obviously has profound implications for the ways goods are regarded and used, since they provide the foundations for value systems and normative frameworks and, through them, attitudes and behaviour.

- ## Social organisation

  Tightly knit family units, in which social roles are bound up with responsibility to the family, will inevitably influence the kinds of products demanded and the ways purchase decisions are made for many types of product.

- ## Political structures

  Through policy, and also through example, the political system sets the agenda for consumption.

- ## Educational system

  Literacy is obviously a key factor in consumer access to information and also to forms of promotional and advertising activity. Also, of course, it is a key means by which consumer tastes and ideas are formed.

- ## Family/Household roles

  Roles in decision making played by family members are one area where culture shapes consumption. Also, the way the household is actually used and regarded are very important for consumption (the modern household actually forms the focus for leisure activity far more than it did in the past).

- ## Cosmology (beliefs, religious/philosophical political ideologies)

  Generalised belief systems are all pervasive, even in societies which consider themselves secularised. Our holidays and gift-giving occasions are formed around the old religious calendar; the foods we eat reflect moral and aesthetic judgements, as much as nutritional good sense. Many religions proscribe particular forms of consumption, from coffee and alcoholic drinks, to 'provocative' clothes or licentious music. In Japan, notions of what advertising should aim to do are quite different and open claims to be 'superior' to other products would be regarded as shocking and in questionable taste.

Aesthetics

What counts as beauty or ugliness is tied into quite specific values and criteria and a marketer must be aware of these in relation to foreign cultures. Marketing to Japan or India, for instance, brings into play different cultural sensitivities on, for example, sex, where attitudes are quite different to those in the West.

Language

The marketing literature is full of examples where marketers committed horrendous 'faux pas' because of ignorance of the subtleties of language. The marketing of 'Cue' toothpaste in French-speaking Canada failed because the brand name sounds exactly like a very rude French colloquialism. The number 4 (shi) in Japanese also serves as the word for death and needs to be avoided. In India, numerology is also part of everyday knowledge, so that numbers have meanings (6, for instance, is 'hijira', the eunuch). Even native English speakers may vary in their usage of a common language. A useful electronic monitoring device for small children has yet to be marketed in the UK, but the US brand name will have to be changed. It is called the 'Little Bugger'.

Advertising slogans then, need to beware of the pitfalls of the local language games; successful slogans may not work in another language or may be unintentionally funny or offensive. Since marketers often struggle to find the right language to talk to their own customers, this is an even greater problem for international marketers.

Customising or Standardising the Communications Mix

Products developed and successfully marketed within one country cannot necessarily be moved *tout court* into an alien market without problems. A product is composed of many different attributes. Physical dimensions, such as shape, colour and smell are obvious, but there are also symbolic and psychological aspects, such as the image or personality of the product, the associations and meanings involved in its name or selling proposition, etc. Entry into a market with a different set of cultural, religious, economic, social and political factors may create, at best, infelicities and, at worst, extreme offence in reactions to part or all of a product concept or marketing mix.

The problem derives from an inherent tension between two important ideas in marketing. Target marketing and segmentation suggest that the way to maximise sales is to identify specific consumer needs and to tailor product appeals specifically to those needs (i.e. to adapt a product for a new foreign market). At the same time, it is clearly impractical to create separate products for every conceivable segment, since it is more profitable (less costly) to produce a standardised product for a larger market segment (composed of different national markets). This is resolved by considering the costs and benefits of alternative marketing strategies and opting for the one offering greatest profitability.

Arguments in favour of product standardisation include *economies of scale* in the following areas.

Production

- Plant probably confined to one country rather than being duplicated.
- Plant expansion may attract 'home' government grants or other support.
- Plant used to maximum capacity offers best return on its costs.
- Exporting rather than difficult licensing deals.

Research and Development

- Product modification, such as that needed to tailor products to specific foreign markets, is costly and time-consuming in an area where resources are always jealously husbanded.

Marketing

- Promotions, which use the same images and themes in advertising, are clearly more cost effective when only the soundtrack or the printed slogan, has to be changed. Similarly, if distribution systems, sales force training, after sales provision and other aspects of the product mix can be standardised, this saves a great deal of money.

Consumer Mobility

- Finding a familiar brand name is important for the growing numbers of travellers moving across what are, in reality, diminishing national boundaries.

Technological Complexity

The microelectronics market illustrates the inherent danger of diversity in technically complex products. Even the endorsement of powerful Japanese companies could not sustain the Betamax VCR system or non-standard PC systems. The international market selected VHS and IBM.

Greater sales, where this also means greater profitability, is the major argument in favour of product adaptation. Varied conditions of product use may force a company to modify its product. These conditions may include:

- climatic variations (corrosion in cars produced for dry climates);
- literacy or skill levels of users (languages which can be used on a computer);
- cultural, social or religious factors (religious or cultural requirements for food products, e.g. Halal slaughtering of New Zealand lamb for Middle Eastern markets or dolphin-friendly tuna catching methods for Europe and the USA.

Variation in Market Factors

Consumer needs are, by their nature, idiosyncratic and there are likely to be distinctive requirements for each group not met by a standard product.

Governmental or Political Influence

Political factors, such as taxation, specific legislation or the pressure of public opinion, may force a company to produce a local product.

Local competition is also an important factor here. Competition, which more clearly understands and seeks to meet the needs of local consumers, is likely to impact upon the way in which a newcomer company deals with the new market.

GLOBAL STARS CAMPAIGNS STILL GOING STRONG

A product may bring in the customers from many different parts of the world – but will the advertising cut the mustard in Bengal and Brixton at the same time? International advertising campaigns often show that good ideas travel well and some have been going strong for longer than the generation of advertising people that are looking after them now!

Zena Fulbody was the first 'Starclens Starlet' in 1932. It was the turn of Gina Lolabright in the early-1960s and, most recently, we have seen the face – and body – of Sherry Stoneboy looking out at us from our cinema, television and poster advertisements, telling us how important *Starclens* has been for her. Sixty-five years on, the *Starclens* campaign shows no sign whatsoever of flagging and has just set a new record as the longest running international advertising campaign in the history of advertising. Over the past five years, as product advantage is copied ever more quickly, advertising agencies have moved to duplicate the phenomenal success of this international advertising campaign – alongside the other notable successes in this area, including Pepcil and Fordes. Sunleverage products, of which *Starclens* has been a 'cash cow' for many years, have all moved in this direction but none shows signs of matching the sprightly star performer.

Launched in 1927 (and in the UK the following year), *Starclens* is now sold in over 70 countries in various parts of the world, with over 3.5 million tonnes of product moved yearly. Out of these, more than 50 countries use centrally produced advertising and communications materials.

The campaign has proved so successful that it has hardly changed since it originated in the USA back in the early 1930s. In those days, Hollywood cinema dominated the world of entertainment. This ceased to be so with the rise of television in the 1950s but, nonetheless, recommendation and endorsement by a big film name seems not to have lost its pulling power.

Morris Klein, the head of advertising at Sunleverage is philosophical.

> *People kept telling me that the star system was dying, and that the appeal of the big names wasn't going to mean as much as it once did. Stars don't carry the same authority, they keep telling me. I just look at the sales figures. Like Bill Goldman says, 'Nobody knows nothin' in this town. Go figure!!*

Klein admits that they have broadened the concept of a star to incorporate the world of television and (more recently) video films. These have become ever more important as the 'target audience' for cinema releases has got younger over the past twenty years. But the general approach is the same as it has always been. The 'Starlet' campaign seems to be a great insurance policy against unstable markets. Although one or two of the sponsors have jumped ship on occasion, generally speaking, the company has been able to maintain possession of its valuable film stars and has kept up the campaign in the face of competitors who would dearly love to take it up.

Away from the obvious improvements in production techniques and changes in the actual stars used over the years, the ways in which the stars are presented is also apparent. It is no longer the case that she simply floats around in a diaphanous ball gown or lounges in the middle of a bath surrounded by bubbles. Tracksuits, casual clothes and sports are the order of the day in the health conscious 1990s. As Klein comments:

> *We want the personality of the star to come through — this is what sells and appeals to our target audience, not just the glamour of the individual.*

Stars are not on pedestals any more, they need to be human and approachable and this has been shown to be one of the biggest factors in their appeal for the past twenty years. This same research reveals that these stars are also held in high esteem and trusted. James Grabbit, senior researcher at J Walter Huston commented:

> *These are still figures who represent the aspirations of a generation. They are to be trusted because they are success incarnate – what they say and what they believe accounts for something amongst the general public.*

Stars of *Beachwatch* and *Beverly Hills Confidential*, Victoria Prince and Beverly Briggs who will figure in coming campaigns, are being surrounded by big-budget spending. Only the best locales and the highest production values will be appropriate, if the use of the stars is to achieve its effect. If the mix is not right, and the resulting film is not good, the companies throughout the world will not buy it: and, surprisingly enough, the kinds of choices made by executives in many parts of the world are based on just the same kinds of reasons.

This is not a one way street, however, the prestige of this long-running campaign is such that, when asked, virtually everyone accepts. Who could turn down a 'role' filled in the past by such distinguished acolytes as Carole Lombitt, Katherine Hepsturn, Ginger Rollins and Michaela Pfeiffs? The then-minor star Sherry Stoneboy found that her career suddenly went into overdrive when she was surprisingly offered the endorsement in 1987.

A related campaign, which has only been going since the early-1970s, but seems likely to last, is the *Instinct* perfume campaign. Originally aimed at late-teens, this campaign has grown with its market and is now targeted at early to mid-twenties. More sophisticated versions of the basic theme are now appearing (influenced by the perfume, a young man 'impulsively' buys flowers or some other extravagant gift, for a passing beauty). The films are not made centrally, so each country tends to display cultural differences in the way the films are made.

Although the giving of flowers, for example, is held to be a European custom, the advertising message of "when a stranger gives you flowers, that's instinct" has been almost universally accepted. Therefore, although some doubts were expressed in a number of different countries, a successful campaign in one country may be transferred to other countries despite apparent cultural barriers.

The gesture has been accepted, but the types and forms of the flowers seem to vary a little. Italians consider one flower more romantic, although in other countries, it is the volume of flowers, which is held to be most appropriate. Some countries will expect the flowers to be grabbed or even stolen from a restaurant or a public park – in others, this would be unacceptable.

The correct cultural interpretation is always available from Personal Goods Connotations, a company which works closely with the advertising agency. This company produces a video and some written guides on how to tell the story they want in the best way for the culture concerned. Important elements will include:

- the man's expression when first struck by the perfume;
- the instinctive gesture when the gift is handed over;
- the girl's expression of surprise;
- the final expression of delight.

The commercial can then be 'customised' for a particular country. Sometimes it doesn't quite work, but most often it does. Sometimes, ideas from smaller countries come to dominate in the process of cross fertilisation, according to Roger Stein, managing director of Personal Goods Connotations.

> *These are often used in countries far from where they are made. Generally, it is best to avoid anything too specific in the way of place references, so that other countries can more easily identify with the situations involved. Occasionally, well-known symbols of a particular nation can be useful, but sometimes, national pride gets in the way, so that neutrality is the best policy with regard to locations at any rate.*

Whenever a commercial is made, local agencies are notified. Extra footage for 'pack shots' and 'body sequences' can be inserted at little extra cost or effort. This is a vital part of transferring commercials from one place to another. For example, places such as Denmark are perfectly tolerant of 'all over' body shots, whereas many other countries will not tolerate any more than the head and neck. These differences simply must be taken into account – or the market will be lost!!!!

9.1. *Planning this campaign for the coming five years, which star would you choose, if any? What would be your reasons?*

9.2. *Describe the main features of the campaign, which have enabled it to be so successful.*

9.3 *Imagine that you wish to run a campaign:*
- *in Iran;*
- *in Saudi Arabia;*
- *in Brazil.*

What problems do you anticipate in formulating an appropriate communication and promotional campaign?

9.4 *What factors may result in the failure of an international marketing campaign? Would you say that marketing communications factors are likely to be the biggest cause of failure? Provide illustrations of areas where international advertising can go wrong.*

9.5 *A Croatian colleague in your advertising agency has expressed interest in producing a film to be used to advertise wines from the south of the newly independent nation. The film will emphasise the low cost and alcoholic content of the wines concerned and he intends to use images of peasant gatherings involving heavy consumption of the wines concerned. Write him a briefing letter, indicating what you think are the five main factors about the wine consumer in your country.*

9.6 *Indicate whether or not you think the proposed theme of the advertising is likely to be acceptable; if not, pose an alternative.*

BIBLIOGRAPHY

Barich, H & Kotler, P, "A Framework for Marketing Image Management" *Sloan Management Review* (Winter 1991) **94** pp. 94-104.

Colley, R, *Defining Advertising Goals for Measured Advertising Results* (New York: Association of National Advertisers) 1961.

Davis, M, "Sales Promotion as a Competitive Strategy" *Management Decision* (1992) **30**(7): pp. 5-10.

Dichter, E, "How Word of Mouth Advertising Works" *Havard Business Review* (Nov/Dec 1966) **44** pp. 147-166.

Engel, J, Blackwell, R *et al.*, *Consumer Behaviour* (San Diego: Dryden Press) 1990.

Fill, C, (1995). *Marketing Communications* (Hemel Hempstead: Prentice Hall) 1995.

Gofton, L R, *Food Fears and Time Famines; Some Social Aspects of Choosing and Using Food* "Why We Eat What We Eat" (London: British Nutrition Foundation 12th Annual Conference, Royal College of Physicians) 1990.

Hovland, C & Mandell, W, "An Experimental Comparison of Conclusion Drawing by the Communicator and the Audience" *Journal of Abnormal and Social Psychology* (July 1952) **47** pp. 581-588.

Hovland, C & Lumsdaine, A *et al.*, *Experiments on Mass Communication* (New York, Wiley) 1949.

Ind, N, *The Corporate Image; Strategies for Effective Identity Programmes* (London: Kogan Page) 1992.

Katz, D, *The Social Psychology of Organizations* (New York: Wiley) 1978.

Kelman, H, "Processes of Opinion Change" *Public Opinion Quarterly* (Spring 1961) **25** pp. 57-78.

Kitchen, P, "Developing use of PR in a Fragmented Demassified Market" *Marketing Intelligence and Planning* (1991) **9**(2) pp. 29-33.

Kitchen, P & Proctor R, "The Increasing Importance of Public Relations in FMCG Firms" *Journal of Marketing Management* (1991) **7** pp. 357-370.

Koten, J, "Car Makers use Image Maps as a Tool to Position Products" *Wall Street Journal* (22 March 1984).

Kotler, P, *Marketing Management; Analysis, Planning and Control* (Englewood Cliffs: New Jersey: Prentice Hall) 1980.

Kotler, P & Mindak W, "Marketing and Public Relation" *Journal of Marketing* (October 1978) **42** pp. 13-20.

Kreigel, R, "How to Choose the Right Communications Objectives" *Business Marketing* (April 1986) pp. 94-106.

Lancaster, G, *Essentials of Marketing* (London: Wiley) 1992.

Lancaster, G & Jobber D, *Selling and Sales Management* (London: Pitman Publishing) 1994.

Lannon, J, "Asking the Right Questions: What do People do with Advertising?" *Admap* (March 1992) pp. 11-16.

Lavidge, R & Steiner G, "A Model for Predictive Measurements of Advertising Effectiveness" *Journal of Marketing* (October 1961).

Mueller-Herman, G, "Market and Technology Shifts in the 1990s: Market Fragmentation and Mass Customization" *Journal of Marketing Management* (1992) **8** pp. 303-314.

Peters, T, *Thriving on Chaos* (New York: Macmillan) 1987.

Porter, M, *Competitive Advantage* (New York: Free Press) 1985.

Schramm, W, *How Communication Works The Process and Effects of Mass Communication* (W Schramm, Urbana, University of Illinois Press) (1955) pp. 3-26.

Shaw & Stone, "Database Marketing" (1988).

Sinclair, S & Stalling E, "Perceptual Mapping; A Tool for Industrial Marketing" *Journal of Business and Industrial Marketing* (1990) **5**(1) pp. 55-65.

Smith, P, *Marketing Communications* (London: Kogan Page) 1993.

Van Raaij, W, "The Effect of Marketing Communication on the Initiation of Juvenile Smoking" *International Journal of Advertising* (1990) **9** pp. 15-16.

Vaughn, R, "How Advertising Works: A Planning Model" *Journal of Advertising Research* (1980) **20**(5) pp. 27-33.

Wells, W & Burnett, J *et al.*, *Advertising: Principles and Practice* (Englewood Cliffs: New Jersey, Prentice Hall) 1989.

Wilmhurst, J, *Below the Line Promotion* (London: Butterworth Heinemann) 1993.

INDEX